Midnight Marquee's

**Reel
Mad
Doctors**

Midnight Marquee's

Reel Mad Doctors

by Gary J. Svehla
Barry Atkinson, William Max Miller and Steven Thornton
Edited by Susan Svehla

Midnight Marquee Press, Inc.
Baltimore, MD

Copyright © 2009 by Gary J. and Susan Svehla
Interior layout by Gary J. Svehla
Cover design by Susan Svehla
Copy Editing by Tom Proveaux

Without limiting the rights under copyright reserved above, no part of this publication may be reproduced, stored in or introduced into a retrieval system, or transmitted, in any form, or by any means (electronic, mechanical, photocopying, recording or otherwise), without the prior written permission of the copyright owner or the publishers of the book.

ISBN 13: 978-1-887664-981
ISBN 10: 1-887664-98-X
Library of Congress Catalog Card Number 2009910822
Manufactured in the United States of America

First Printing by Midnight Marquee Press, Inc., October 2009

**Dedicated to
MidMar's loyal readers**

TABLE OF CONTENTS

8   **Introduction**

9   **An A to Z Guide To Reel Mad Doctors**

63   **Bride of Frankenstein and The Legacy of Dr. Pretorius by William Max Miller**

71   **Our Favorite Mad Doctors**

80   **Karloff: The Maddest Doctor of All??? The Devil Commands vs. The Man Who Changed His Mind**

90   **If I Only Had a Brain !!! by Steven Thornton**

When it comes to the icons of the horror/science fiction film genre, the popularly coined phrase "Mad Doctors" becomes one essential component of just what makes horror movies so fantastic. For every popular monster, behind each skulking, hulking terror, lies one or more monster makers, usually audacious men (and more frequently, women) of science who dare to dabble in God's domain. Whether these whack cases are attempting to create new life from sewing together assorted body parts of the dead, restore disfigurement to normalcy, mount an army of monsters capable of conquering the world or maintain youth and vitality and thus avoid the deteriorating rigors of old age and death, our favorite mad doctors always forge new avenues of discovery. Sometimes inflated egos or fragile psyches cause anti-social behavior to dominate; these mad docs put their intelligence, self-serving causes and means-justify-the-ends mentality front and center. Some such scientists are hated and feared, while others arouse our sense of sympathy and hope. But as far as movies go, mad docs drive the world of horror cinema and often become just as charismatic as the evil fiends they create.

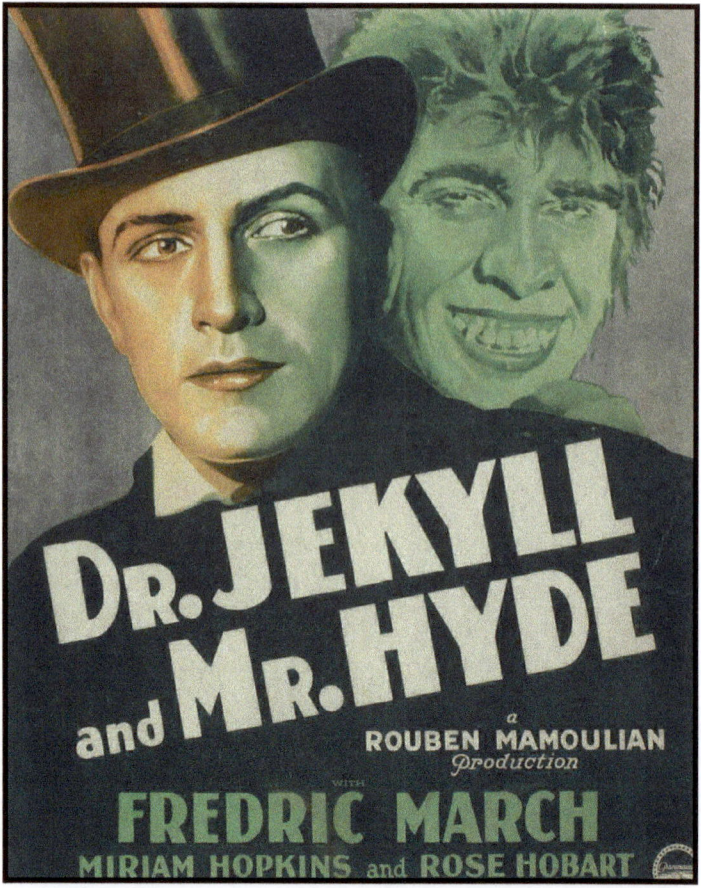

Basically, three modes of mad scientists exist in horror cinema, all worthy of our attention. First, we have the Dr. Frankenstein and all his clones, scientists who are twisted, anti-social and obsessive, doctors that invade God's domain and plan to forward their brand of knowledge for better or worse. Most such mad scientists rant that theie create will benefit the world of science—not necessarily the world of humanity. Their new blend of knowledge is like a fetus, ready to be born nine months along, nothing can stop it from happening; and like the force of nature that such knowledge has become, the scientist will sacrifice anyone or anything to achieve his labor of a lifetime. The second type of scientist is, for example, Dr. Delambre of 1958's *The Fly*, a great mind interested in using new technology to benefit mankind, but alas, something goes awry. Perhaps the scientist makes an error or miscalculation, and what should be benevolent suddenly becomes evil. (Who would have thought that a housefly would have invaded Delambre's integrator transport machine!!!!) In such movies we the audience feel sympathy and remorse for the scientist-as-victim, but when Al Hedison comes out of his re-integrator machine with the head and arm of a household fly, all we can do is cower in fear, scream our heads off and run for the exits. In this second mad doc category, we focus on the scientist that becomes the victim of super-science. Third, we have the brilliant yet totally demented man of science, one who uses his scientific mind to create only evil. Think of Bela Lugosi as Dr. Carruthers from *The Devil Bat*. Carruthers works for an insensitive corporation that profits by the millions, while the humble doctor gets thrown small bonus checks once in a while to assuage the company's guilt. Carruthers soon cracks and turns his scientific mind to vengeance and punishment. Yes, yes yes, corporate executives often deserve their comeuppance, but do they deserve to have a new formula after-shave lotion thrown on their exposed necks, after-shave that will attract a lab-bred giant devil bat to rip their throats apart! Sometimes a mad scientist can only accept so much abuse until he/she turns science against humanity. Most cinematic mad docs are one of these three stereotypes, or a combination of them.

Here at last is a celebration of the mad doctor in the movies. Our goal is not to cover every movie that featured a mad scientist, but simply to celebrate the archetypal character (in all manifestations) in some of the most profound movies that featured mad doctors in prominent roles. Author Gregory Mank celebrated *Hollywood's Maddest Doctors*, citing George Zucco, Lionel Atwill and Colin Clive as the progenitors of mad lab terror. This book does not disagree, but here we try to broaden the scope of investigating mad doctors and look at the films, not just the actors and the delightful characters they created. The bottom line is this—where would the monster, mutant or creeping terror be without its creator? As movies teach us in such instances, it takes two to tango and terror from beyond often cannot come to reality without the active participation of the dreaded mad doc—the deluded mind that precipitates all the mayhem. In the world of fantastic cinema, it's such evil minds that we celebrate!

—Gary J. Svehla
August 2009

An A to Z Guide To
Reel Mad Doctors

The Alligator People
20th Century Fox, 1959; Director: Roy del Ruth

Back in 1959, a B horror movie in black and white and CinemaScope was something rather special. Such a widescreen horror film with its denser, far-reaching tapestry of mood, monsters and fright upped the ante of the production.

Roy Del Ruth, one of the oldest directors working in Hollywood at the time, created an old-style horror romp (even using Karl Struss as cinematographer) for the new pop art generation…men turned into alligators (old school "weregators") through the use of an alligator serum and a radiation machine created in an atomic laboratory (new school science). Veterans Frieda Inescort, Lon Chaney, Jr., George Macready and Bruce Bennett joined new upstarts Richard Crane (graduating from the *Rocky Jones* TV series) and Beverly Garland (most recently an American International heroine, working for Roger Corman).

This programmer deals with dual losses of identity. First in the framing story, young and lovely Beverly Garland has repressed her former life of horror, and only through hypnosis can she recall her marriage to Richard Crane and the nightmare they encountered, leading to the gruesome death of her husband in the bayou. By the movie's end the doctors decide it is best that her past life remain forgotten. Richard Crane's character, that of a former military flyer who broke every bone in his body from a horrible plane crash, received experimental treatments at his mother's plantation deep in Louisiana swamp country. However, while on a train honeymooning with Garland, Crane receives a wire with such bad news (he is losing his human identity) that he immediately abandons his wife and leaves the train at its first available stop. The wily and also deeply-in-love Garland traces him to his home and faces horror she never imagined.

First of all, we are treated to an over-the-top but juicy Lon Chaney, Jr. supporting characterization, as a bayou bumpkin who lost one hand to the "slimy gators," and is now forced to wear a hook. His hatred for the alligators seems secondary to the passion he feels for the sexy Garland, whose face he lustfully rubs with his steel hook. Pretty soon Chaney, Jr. is preying upon both the gators and the not-interested Garland. Chaney, Jr.'s performance is too broad and overall ridiculous, yet it is definitely a memorable performance that children fondly remember.

Richard Crane probably submits the performance of his career here, as the brooding and frightened macho husband, who cannot share his personal swamp demons with his new wife. At the plantation, Crane's character is still human, although his face and arms have taken on the roughness of alligator skin, as his treatments are turning him into something quasi-human. Crane, fearing for his humanity, forces scientist George Macready to use the full dose of his radiation treatments to either cure or kill him, but Chaney, Jr.'s interference (and striking death by electrocution caused by his metal hook touching an electrical apparatus in the lab) results in the house exploding…but not before Crane is transformed into an actual weregator whose former soft skin becomes alligator tough, and his face and head erupt into a large alligator snoot. The makeup is pure rubber suit and looks it; however, the actual makeup concept is pretty imaginative for a 1959 B programmer. Within minutes of wife Beverly Garland seeing her husband's transformation and screaming her head off, the Crane gator walks into quicksand and submerges, far too quickly.

The Alligator People, a favorite of mine as a kid, features stark mood, fog-shrouded set design and haunting

A foreign movie poster from *The Awful Doctor Orlof*

CinemaScope photography. The performances, mostly by tried-and-true veterans, are more than effective, and the monster makeup delivers the goods. The film's only flaw is a too leisurely pace with the need for one or two additional shocking payoff sequences. But for a late 1950s matinee romp, *The Alligator People* entertains.

Gary J. Svehla

The Awful Doctor Orlof
Hispamer/Sigma, 1962; Director: Jesus Franco

The first Spanish horror movie and the initiator of over 300 Hispanic sci-fi/horror pictures up to the mid-1970s, Franco's groundbreaking surgical thriller drew its references from everything that had gone before—1919's *The Cabinet of Dr. Caligari*, the Expressionist German cinema of the 1920s, Carl Dreyer's *Vampyr*, the Universal horror flicks of the 1930s and 1940s and Hammer's output of the 1950s. But with the mix came liberal doses of nudity, sadism, sexual sleaze and brutality, to create a unique European sub-genre of medical, semi-pornographic horror that would eventually evolve into the slasher films of the 1970s and 1980s. The plot became so popular with Spanish, French and Italian audiences that similar plots appeared in scores of films and sequels, such as *The Secret of Doctor Orloff* (1964) and *The Diabolical Dr. Z* (1965); even the British had a go at it with *Corruption* (1967). Murder became a kind of eroticism, tapping into areas of the psyche that others had only dared hint at, reaching its zenith in Mario Bava's *Blood and Black Lace* and Ricardo Freda's *The Horrible Dr. Hichcock*. Here Howard Vernon is a mad doctor kidnapping a constant stream of young dancers to experiment on, as his disfigured daughter requires new skin to cover her scarred features (ah, the plot can be traced back to *Eyes Without A Face*). Like Jack the Ripper (the action takes place in 1912), Vernon stalks the shadowy, rain-swept streets in his cloak with Morpho, his mute, blind assistant, whom he rescued from the gallows seven years previously. Although the lecherous Morpho, with eyes like hard-boiled eggs, is as blind as a bat, he still manages to grab hold of the nubile showgirls, vampirizing them until they are dead, before Vernon carries out his experiments in his Gothic castle. True to form, the grafts refuse to take, as the unwilling donors have been killed beforehand, so live, human lab rats are needed. The unfortunate girls are chained up in the castle's dungeons for use in one experiment after another, until they expire. Two occurrences contribute to Vernon's downfall—he stabs his female assistant to death (Morpho worshipped the woman) and his next intended victim happens to be the girlfriend of the local police inspector, who is investigating the kidnappings. When the police find Morpho's coffin empty, the inspector, with the help of a petty thief, locates Vernon's castle across a river and shoots Morpho (who has strangled his master for killing his beloved mistress) from the battlements, his girlfriend having escaped the operating table. Franco's surrealistic camerawork (shot from all manner of bizarre angles), his use (sometimes overuse) of zoom, artful back lighting in the street scenes and stark black-and-white photography set the tone for things to come. Let's not forget that quirky, discordant soundtrack either, full of drums and pipes, another hallmark of these continental thrillers. Released under various titles (*The Demon Doctor*, *The Diabolical Dr. Satan* and *Cries in the Night*), the uncut 90-minute original with subtitles is hard to locate. Most versions run 86-minutes, featuring terrible dubbing and several gratuitously violent scenes edited from the print for its initial U.K. and U.S. release. *The Awful Dr. Orlof* is a trendsetting horror picture that all students of European cinema should have in their collection—to watch, to enjoy and to study Franco's virtuoso techniques to the fullest.

Barry Atkinson

Beast of Blood
Hemisphere, 1971; Director: Eddie Romero

It's hard to believe that people a generation younger than me love the *Beast of Blood* trilogy for the same reasons that I love Richard Cunha's *Frankenstein's Daughter*. Schlock B programmers such as *Frankenstein's Daughter* offer a sense of fun and style, allowing me to relive a more innocent time. Oddly enough, John Ashley, the actor who looks like a squat Elvis Presley, sneer and all, stars in both B productions, and Ashley still appears handsome in this cult classic.

What cheapens the appeal of *Beast of Blood* is its island location, with its abundance of frightened natives looking gloomy, and its too-often used long, dull treks through the monsters are classic in the best 1950s sense, and Eddie Garcia's performance as Lorca is far too short but highly effective. If only the pacing were faster and the plot better constructed, this film might have been its generation's *Frankenstein's Daughter*.

While never a favorite of mine, I must admit that *Beast of Blood* does have its moments.

Gary J. Svehla

Black Friday
Universal, 1940; Director: Arthur Lubin

While *Black Friday* is rare enough and deserves the restored DVD release given it in the *Bela Lugosi Collection*, I would have much preferred an even rarer title to be included. But *Black Friday* offers Karloff and Lugosi in performances that were changed a short while before production began. So Stanley Ridges, as the benevolent college professor who inherits the brain of a criminal mastermind, steals the show. Bela Lugosi, puffy-faced and wearing black, brings a less than original take to the 1940s gangster arena with his portrayal of Eric Marnay. And the stereotypical and sympathetic Dr.

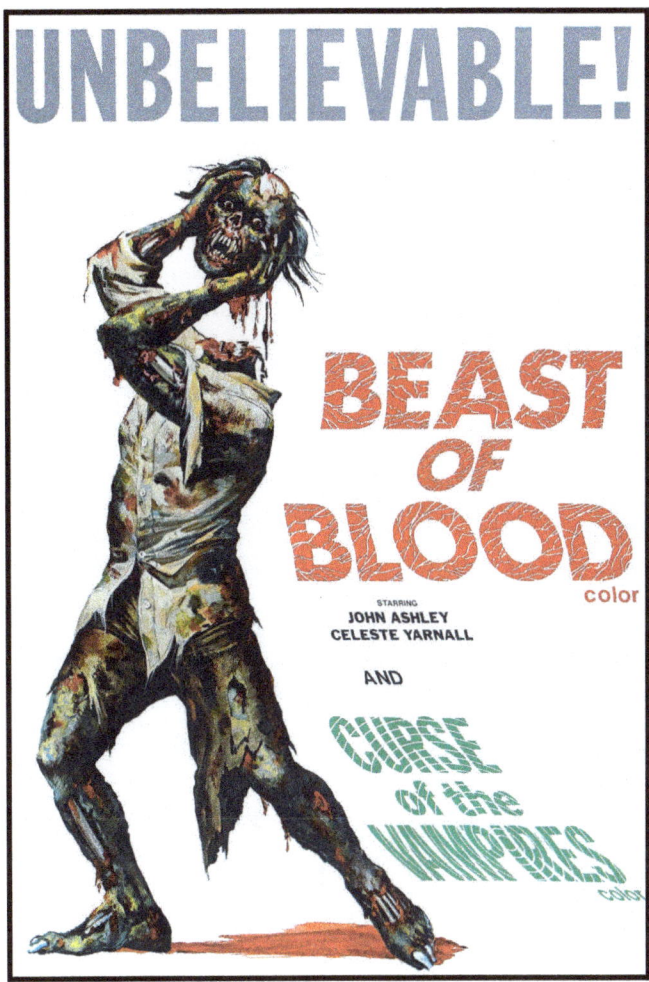

jungle, over the rocky bluffs, across the beach. The plot is meandering and padded, but the monster attacks are numerous and, especially when the Ashley party finds and explores the deserted mansion of the evil Dr. Lorca (Eddie Garcia), the mood becomes creepy and frightening. The shots of dead green-blooded monsters, maggots crawling over their decaying flesh, are unsettling. The other American cast member, Celeste Yarnall (TV appearances include *Star Trek* and *It Takes a Thief*), even has a gratuitous nude sequence and she loves to parade around in her island jungle bikini, even after Lorca's men hold her captive.

This all leads to the ridiculous final third, when we come across the still-surviving Lorca (he was badly burned in the fiery conclusion of the previous entry), who has decapitated his beast of blood in an attempt to control its killing instinct. Just like in *Re-Animator*, both the body and the head of the fiend are kept alive, and when the body breaks free of its straps, the head begins to moan menacingly, "Lorca, I will talk now," as the two-piece monster destroys the scientist's lab and again sets the island ablaze.

To be honest, when *Beast of Blood* is in its most creepy mode (such as the attack upon the sleeping Yarnall, as one of the green-blooded fiends sneaks slowly into the house, taking its time before attacking her), it is gripping and fun. The

Sovac presents Boris Karloff with another by-the-numbers performance that shines by nature of the actor's overwhelming talent. The film works best in its opening minutes when we see Sovac, framed by prison bars and sitting in the shadows, awaiting his execution for murder. As he passes a young reporter on his long walk to oblivion, he hands his notebook to him. Sovac tells the young man that the reporter's newspaper presented the fairest coverage of the trial, and, in a handwritten note, he wishes his research will serve the needs of mankind. Sadly, the benevolently mad Sovac is paying with his own life for saving the life of his best friend, even though to save him he had to transfer the mind of a criminal into his friend. The zippy quick-cuts punctuated with crescendoing musical cues give *Black Friday* a unique visual style that is all but forgotten once the movie becomes a standard story told in flashbacks.

Black Friday would have been better if Karloff or Lugosi portrayed the professor role enacted by Ridges, but the truth is that Ridges probably played the role better than either icon, and this fact seems to anger most critics who view the film as somewhat of an aborted effort. As released, Lugosi is little more than supporting player and Karloff delivers a performance that fails to even challenge him. Ridges creates a Jekyll and Hyde bravura performance, while the two horror icons are reduced to bland support. It is impossible to watch *Black Friday* and not think about what other role Karloff and Lugosi should be playing. It's not that *Black Friday* is bad; it is simply generic. Yes, it is probably better than *The Mad Ghoul* because of its star power and extra budget, but it's barely better. After *The Raven*, *The Black Cat* and *The Invisible Ray,* fans expected and deserved better. The real crime of *Black Friday* is watching two horror film icons being upstaged by a supporting player.

Gary J. Svehla

The Black Sleep
United Artists, 1956; Director: Reginald LeBorg

Although made in the 1950s, *The Black Sleep* has far more of a 1940s feel to it, although the graphic piece of brain surgery midway into the film wouldn't have been allowed in that decade. The year is 1872. Basil Rathbone gives a commanding performance as ruthless Dr. Cadman, experimenting on the various functions of the brain in order to cure his beautiful wife of a brain tumor. The woman has been in a coma for eight months and is on the verge of dying. To place his unknowing "subjects" into the trance necessary for him to carry out his experiments, he administers to them an ancient East Indian cataleptic drug named "Nind Andhera," which suspends all signs of life in a person's body. By using the potion, he rescues promising student Herbert Rudley (serving time in London's Newgate Prison, on a trumped-up murder charge) from the hangman's noose and bamboozles him into helping with his illegal operations. Sleazy Akim Tamiroff supplies the doctor with more unwilling persons to tamper with. But unbeknown to Rudley, several unfortunate victims of Rathbone's botched experiments are chained in the cellar of his mansion, although strangely, two of them are allowed to wander around the house—Lon Chaney, Jr. as demented strangler Mungo, whose murderous nature is kept in check by Rathbone's nurse, and a very old-looking Bela Lugosi as a mute servant (it was the morphine-addicted actor's last full role; he died shortly after the movie was released). Rudley rebels against what he sees as Rathbone's unethical methods and then, with a young girl assistant, stumbles across the freaks in the cellar—John Carradine as a skinny, deranged prophet; Tor Johnson playing his usual blank-eyed, heavyweight mutant; a horribly scarred sailor; and a deranged woman. They all break free of their chains in the end and go after the doctor, just as Rathbone is about to perform another brain operation on Rudley's girlfriend. Chaney, Jr. the

strangler is strangled himself, Rathbone and his wife fall to their deaths from a stairway and Rudley (plus girlfriend) is pardoned as a free man. Flatly directed by LeBorg, the film still scores as an effective piece of full-blooded horror fare because of Rathbone's dominating turn, an array of horrible-looking deviants to satisfy the fans, Les Baxter's noisy music and the poignant sight of a shambling Lugosi, one of horror's true legends, in his final starring role.

Barry Atkinson

Blood of Dracula
AIP, 1957; Director: Herbert L. Strock

Most mad doctors in the movies are men, but sometimes the female of the species has the opportunity to demonstrate intelligent evil as well. Poor teenager Nancy Perkins (Sandra Harrison) becomes the sympathetic victim of evil. After the death of her mother and her father's sudden remarriage, Nancy finds herself shipped off to a private girl's school, where she has to fend for herself in the world of female teenage politics. Nancy pretends to be a badass, but she is lonely and confused and feels rejected. Her intimidating science teacher Miss Branding (Louise Lewis), with an evil agenda all her own, takes the vulnerable and angry teen under her wing. After Nancy is injured in a science lab experiment, due to the shenanigans of nasty student Nola (Heather Ames), Miss Branding places Nancy in a trance, seemingly to eliminate her physical pain, but also to put the girl under her control, using an ancient amulet rescued from the Carpathian Mountains (referencing Count Dracula, of course). Branding has a theory involving regression that she wants to prove, and the cold-as-ice educator feels that sacrificing one individual for the sake of science is acceptable. Soon, in a quivering, eerie transformation, the pretty student morphs into a horrible hag with fangs, who attacks at night (including her nemesis Nola, of course) the student population, Nancy is now a slave to her lab-created vampirism.

The strength of this exploitative American International production is that the movie transcends the formula to produce a chilling and sensitive portrait of teenage angst (the movie serves as a female counterpart to the similar and equally effective *I Was a Teenage Werewolf*). Even though Nancy projects a hard shell to the adults and teens in her life, we can see she is a victim of all the crap outside school. The predatory Miss Branding notices immediately that the troubled teen needs both guidance and a mentor, an adult who takes the time to care about her. And while Branding is anyone but that person, Branding is clever enough to gain the girl's trust so that the young victim can be used for Branding's devious experiments. The transformations and nighttime stalkings are cleverly photographed and edited for maximum chills, and the vampire attacks are as good as any in the AIP canon. But it is the sensitive and damaged-goods performance by Sandra Harrison that makes her character so compelling. By the movie's end, Nancy has figured out that she is the monstrous fiend on campus, and when she confronts the actual monster, Miss Branding, Nancy's anger results in another transformation, a final one, where she attacks and kills her teacher, justice finally being served before the teen monster also meets a bitter end.

I Was a Teenage Werewolf and *Blood of Dracula* are my two favorite American International black-and-white drive-in horror movies, but while the mad doctors in *I Was a Teenage Werewolf* are interesting (Whit Bissell shines in both that film and *I Was a Teenage Frankenstein*), Louise Lewis creates a dazzling performance of female empowerment gone berserk in *Blood of Dracula*—in the name of science of course.

Gary J. Svehla

Brain of Blood (aka The Undying Brain)
Hemisphere, 1972; Director: Al Adamson

In 1972 Hemisphere Pictures did not have a new Philippine monstrosity to loose upon the drive-in world, so Eddie Romero hired Sam Sherman and Al Adamson to produce a quickie drive-in feature that could fill the bill and satisfy the fans. What Sherman and Adamson loosed upon the unsuspecting masses was *Brain of Blood* (maintaining the profitable "blood" motif), a movie whose style is based upon generic low-budget ineptness. Once again we have a movie

becomes the final resting place for the brain. Of course "big hair" Regina Carroll (the wife of Al Adamson) plays the woman that needs to keep the ruler's brain alive—so he can marry her and make her co-ruler of his nation.

The movie itself is slow-paced, predictable and mostly silly, but it does feature a few interesting sequences, and the cast of veterans is always interesting to watch, if sometimes in an embarrassing can-you-believe-this way. However, Sam Sherman and Al Adamson did deliver a Hemisphere product that was ready-made for the drive-in circuit, and considering what it must have cost, was a success for all concerned.

The film is not really my cup of tea, but for fans of 1970s exploitation, *Brain of Blood* has acquired cult following.

Gary J. Svehla

Bride of the Monster
Banner/DCA, 1955; Director: Edward D. Wood, Jr.

This is one of the King of the Awful's most notorious grade Z efforts, so, if you can abandon reality and accept certain facts, then this tatty production under Wood's direction isn't all *that* incompetent (take a look at *Robot Monster*, for instance). First, that an aging Bela Lugosi puts his heart and soul (as well as a hammy bit of overacting) into the role of scientist Dr. Varnoff, a madman that wants to create a race of atomic-powered super beings via his atomic ray machine (Lugosi desperately needed the wages as well). Second, that the atomic ray machine is a badly fitting tin hat with two electrodes sprouting from the top. Third, that lumbering Tor Johnson as Lobo barges through a door and the whole set shakes. Fourth, that the fake rubber octopus (filched supposedly from Paramount's property department), which Lugosi tangles with, doesn't move an inch; Fifth, that Wood's night scenes are so dark you cannot fathom out what is going on or who is who. Sixth, that the Chief of Police (Harvey Dunn) sits in his office with a canary perched on his left shoulder. Seventh, that liberal use of stock footage bolsters up the running time to 69 minutes. Eighth, that when Lugosi's lab explodes in the climax footage of an atom bomb is inserted, and that if it were a real bomb, the bomb's intensity would have annihilated cast, crew and the whole of Los Angeles. Ninth, that there are far too many close-ups of Lugosi's mesmerizing eyes. Tenth, that Lobo is shot about 12 times yet still staggers around with no ill-effects (and no bullet holes) and atomic-powered Lugosi is shot about *20* times and staggers around without any ill effects. Eleventh, that Tony McCoy, as a detective, fights grainy stock footage of a marauding alligator. So, if you can suspend disbelief and totally accept the usual (and legendary) parade of Wood's inadequacies, continuity errors and gaffes, what you have is an extremely amateurish horror movie (unbelievably, it was X-rated in Britain) boosted by a noisy, half-decent score that in its own unique fashion is quite enjoyable. Tune in to Tim Burton's *Ed Wood* one day to see the making of *Bride of the Monster*, and you'll appreciate it just that little bit more!

Barry Atkinson

that screams no budget, but Sherman enjoyed giving old Hollywood veterans a chance to shine again. In this movie we have Kent Taylor as the maniacal mad scientist, who wishes to prove that brain transplants are feasible, Grant Williams (the hero of *The Incredible Shrinking Man*) as another doctor (but Williams is hardly recognizable with his Beatles-style haircut and extra bulk added to his frame), Reed Hadley as a dying/transplanted Middle Eastern ruler and Angelo Rossitto as the vertically-challenged medical assistant. The Sherman/Adamson team has concocted a homage to 1940s schlock, but with an added heavy dose of visceral violence.

In one captivating dungeon sequence the two girls are chained to the wall, both victims slowly being drained of their blood. The evil Angelo Rossitto comes down to take another vial of blood and dangles the keys in front of the ladies as he rants, raves and taunts them, all the while laughing uncontrollably. Instead of transplanting the Middle Eastern ruler's brain into a physically comparable human subject, the wily doctor uses his developmentally-challenged burn-victim assistant, the giant, hulking John Bloom (he played the Frankenstein monster in *Dracula vs. Frankenstein*), as the recipient of the ruler's brain. Of course this will never work and by film's end the poor unfortunate Grant Williams

Captive Wild Woman
Universal, 1943; Director Edward Dmytryk

1943's *Captive Wild Woman* becomes the oddest Universal hybrid of them all: The mad scientist meets the circus. Along with *Man Made Monster*, *Captive Wild Woman* is one of Universal's best B productions and entertains because of its cross-genre action approach. Up and coming Edward Dmytryk directs, and his audacious style, combining wild animal circus action with mad scientist human-to-animal glandular hijinks, produces 61 minutes of horrific thrills. It does not hurt to have John Carradine heading up the cast as Dr. Sigmund Walters, the misguided doctor, who believes it is acceptable to sacrifice human lives in the name of scientific advancement. Once again Evelyn Ankers plays the leading lady, Beth, whose ill sister (Martha MacVicar) is under the treatment of Dr. Walters for a glandular disorder. Oddly, Milburn Stone portrays the dashing leading man, a wild animal trainer, who is not afraid to step inside a cage with ferocious lions and tigers, poised to rip him apart. Not the obvious choice to play such a role, Stone's casting was based mostly on his physical similarity to Clyde Beatty, whose actual wild animal taming stock footage becomes the dramatic impetus for the entire film. Even though if we look closely, it is easy to see that Beatty is not Stone, and vice versa, when caught up in all the action, the two actors blend seamlessly into one.

And non-actor Acquanetta makes her screen debut here, the beauty from Burma, her exotic features make her appear as though she could be an actual evolution of ape into woman. While Acquanetta does not deliver many lines, she is required to react in close up, and that she does with poise and enthusiasm. Say what you may, but Acquanetta was not hired for her thespic talents, but for her looks. For what she is required to do, Acquanetta does a more than credible job as Paula the Ape Woman, and her otherworldly persona suits the film perfectly.

John Carradine is at his best in his small operating room, speaking to his surgical nurse, as she chastises him for daring to sacrifice the lives of innocent victims for his work, and with a glimmer in his eye, at this precise moment, realizes that her brain would be perfect for his glandular operation.

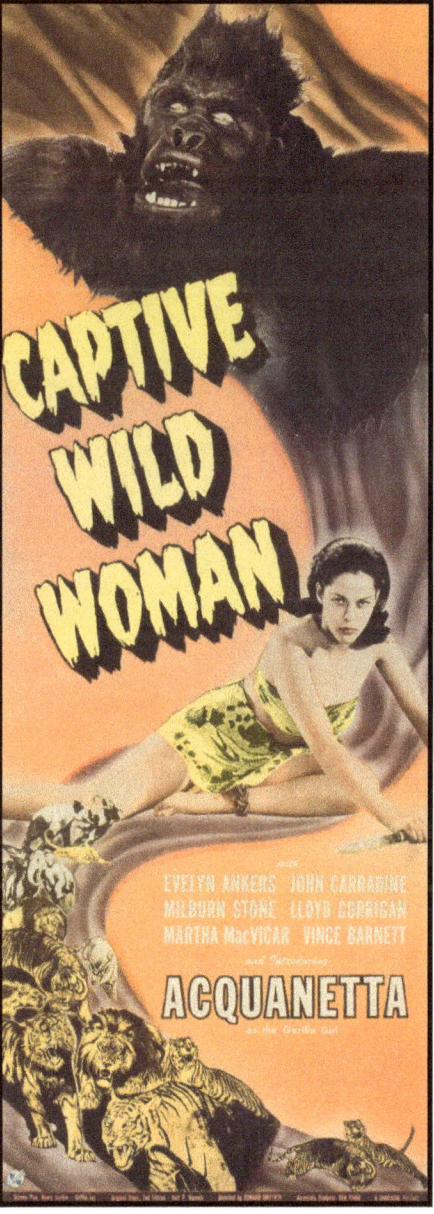

Sacrificing her for the cause of science (and also shutting her up for good) is an easy solution to her nagging. Carradine, almost looking dashing and handsome in a smarmy way, becomes the archetype mad scientist and submits one of his best B performances.

Perhaps the film achieves its B classic status when Fred Mason (Stone), who is dependent upon Paula to control the wild animals when he is in the cage, canoodles with the real woman of his desires, Beth, making Paula insanely jealous. After witnessing the lovey-dovey exchange between the two, Paula returns to her dressing room and tears it apart in anger. She believed that Fred really loved her, but now her heart is broken and her anger fuse ignited. Such an emotional rage regresses the glandular operation that Dr. Walters performed, turning Paula from her beautiful exotic self into a wereape, a female beast with furry hands and claws and a simian face. Dr. Walters announces he has to sacrifice yet another person to return Paula to full humanity, and that sacrifice, of course, happens to be Dorothy, sister of Beth. However, the wild climax results in the caged ape getting loose and creating havoc in the lab, with the good guys coming out on top.

Captive Wild Woman is generally given short shrift, with actress Acquanetta becoming the Universal whipping-girl, second only to Rondo Hatten as Universal horror's worse performer. However, Acquanetta does exactly what is required of her and does it effectively. *Captive Wild Woman* might not be a gem, but it is most definitely a programmer worth watching.

Gary J. Svehla

Circus of Horrors
Paramount, 1960; Director: Sidney Hayers

As can be seen with movies such as *Flesh and the Fiends, Blood of the Vampire* and *Burn, Witch, Burn*, Hammer Film Productions was not the only horror factory turning out Gothic horror movies in Britain in the 1950s and 1960s. *Circus of Horrors*, starring Anton Diffring, directed by Sidney Hayers (*Burn, Witch, Burn*), with a screenplay by George Baxt, has always been a guilty pleasure, suggesting the European perversions that would haunt the screen in the latter half of the 1960s and throughout the 1970s. Featuring splashy EastmanColor photography

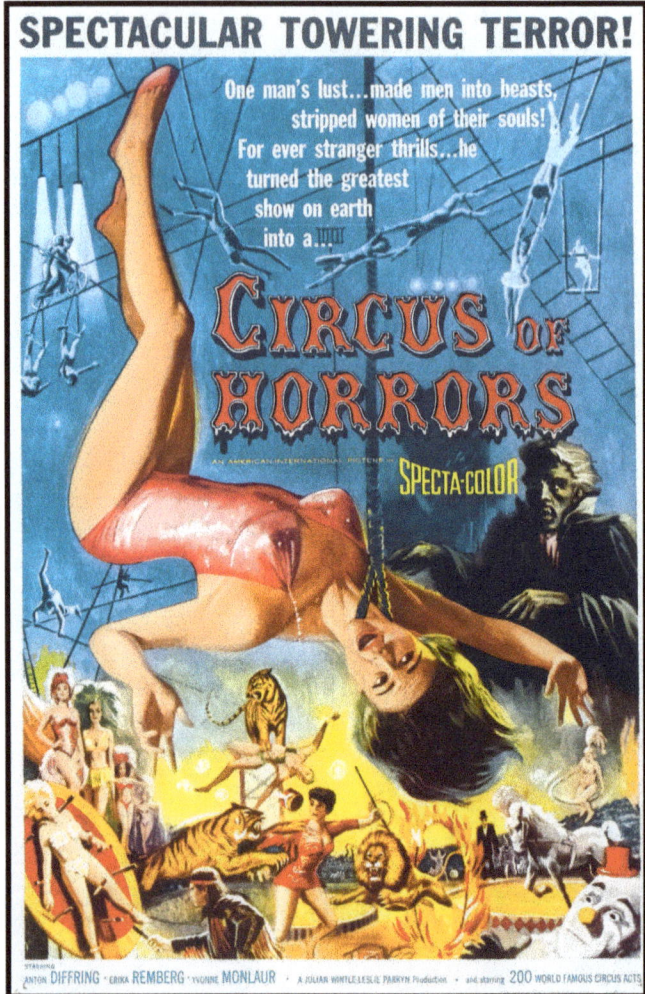

(looking like Technicolor at its most delightfully garish) and a very over-the-top story, showcasing beautiful women, who were formerly disfigured, *Circus of Horrors* becomes the bad-boy British horror production that Hammer has always been accused of being. Think of *The Hypnotic Eye* in color, with a circus motif, and that comes close to describing what *Circus of Horrors* is all about.

The movie's dominant strength is a wonderful villainous performance by Anton Diffring, perhaps his best performance ever, as evil surgeon Dr. Rossiter, who changes his name (to Dr. Schuler) when the police get wind of his radical medical experiments—using new methods of plastic surgery. Escaping to the confines of a small European circus, Rossiter operates on the war-disfigured face of the young daughter of the circus' owner (Donald Pleasence), and when the operation restores the child's beauty, Rossiter is made co-owner of the operation. However Rossiter wants more and inherits the circus by sinister means. Ten years pass and the little girl grows up to be Yvonne Monlaur, in a reddish-blonde wig, looking as beautiful as ever and calling Rossiter "uncle." In these intervening years, the circus has become a haven of beautiful women, most of them coming from a sordid life of crime or prostitution, whose facial scars are corrected and who opt to join the circus, each victim strangely having an exploitable circus talent. Whenever one of the star attractions desires to leave the circus, an unfortunate accident occurs, leaving the now-beautiful woman dead.

Diffring, who himself is scarred by a gorilla near the end of the movie, is surrounded by a bevy of beauties, including the before-mentioned Yvonne Monlaur, Erika Remberg, Yvonne Romain and others. Diffring is equally adept at handling wild animals or enraged, vengeful women...and he is just as skilled at the art of manipulation and deception as he is at using his stiletto knife, which he brandishes with the speed of a python. Wonderful moments occur throughout including a scene where a woman falls from a suspended rope, her crumpled body is covered in blankets on the emergency cot, blood drips from her mouth as Rossiter and cronies dangle on the high-wire above. The nearly dead beauty is feverously attempting to mouth the words that Schuler is actually Rossiter. Or, the fitting climax where Diffring stabs a gorilla, as well as his accomplice, to death, stays three steps ahead of the police that are chasing him through the big tent, only to be mowed down by an automobile driven by a vengeful victim from his past. And yes, that wonderful pop song, "Look for a Star," is played at every opportunity, obviously an attempt to lure in the younger generation...but such an uncool song for the time (although it is catchy!). Anton Diffring becomes one of the classic mad doctors of the decade.

Gary J. Svehla

Climax Mystery Theater: Dr. Jekyll and Mr. Hyde
CBS, July 28, 1955; Director Allen Reisner

Michael Rennie, who died too young, had been receiving substandard roles toward the end of his life, is best known for portraying the alien visitor in *The Day the Earth Stood Still*. During the era of early television, Michael Rennie attempted the dual-character role of good vs. evil in a television version of Robert Louis Stevenson's *Dr. Jekyll and Mr. Hyde*. What survived is a kinescope (a movie made by filming off a TV monitor, as the show was broadcast live) that varies in quality—the print is slightly dark and the focus is soft. However, for a kinescope, the quality is quite acceptable. Sir Cedric Hardwicke (with terminal bags beneath his eyes that rival Lon Chaney, Jr.'s) portrays Jekyll's friend Utterson, who puts the pieces of the puzzle together.

Structurally, this re-telling of the Stevenson classic is interesting—Mr. Hyde dies in the opening sequence. Then Utterson explores Dr. Jekyll's journal and the tale is retold, ending up at the beginning when Utterson has figured out that the corpse before him is no longer Mr. Hyde but the formerly genteel Dr. Jekyll.

Michael Rennie's performance is effective and between both characters he displays a wide range of emotions. The makeup transformation is done quite well for television, with a darkening of the skin, a thickening of eyebrows and the application of a thicker nose and rougher-looking skin, symbolizing the change from good to evil. Rennie's Jekyll lacks the do-gooding overkill of Fredric March's similarly obsessed doctor, although Rennie's Hyde, while effectively achieving a rhythm and buoyance differentiating his Hyde from his Jekyll, never achieves the classic inventiveness of March's Hyde. Rennie is best in the bar sequence, where he changes character without benefit of drugs, and this transformation truly mesmerizes, rendered with simple TV special effects and passionate performing.

Too often the production is waylaid by a reliance upon cinematic tricks from earlier, superior productions. For instance, when Jekyll first transforms into Hyde, the audience sees the transformation from the vantage point of a mirror, and when Jekyll first looks at himself as Hyde, so too does the audience first see Hyde from the point of view of Jekyll looking into the mirror.

For a 50-minute television production, *Dr. Jekyll and Mr. Hyde* is produced adequately and nicely acted by all concerned. While Michael Rennie does not threaten the reputations of Fredric March or Spencer Tracy, but his performance is worthy of note. The creaky early television production and the kinescope presentation do not help matters, but for such a rare piece of cinematic history, preservation in any condition is welcome.

Gary J. Svehla

The Corpse Vanishes
Monogram, 1942; Director: Wallace Fox

Bela Lugosi starred in nine pictures for Poverty Row studio Monogram in the 1940s, and this was one of the better of the nine, released in England as *The Case of the Missing Brides*. Thanks to Fox's fast-paced direction, the short 64-minute running time doesn't lag for an instant as mad scientist Lugosi attempts to keep his 80-year-old wife (a countess) alive by pumping her full of glandular fluid mixed with a serum secreted from the comatose bodies of virgin brides, either stolen from the morgue (where they are believed dead) or on their way to the coroner's office. After a dose of the serum, the withered countess is restored to her once natural beauty. (And this is 14 years before Riccardo Freda's *I Vampiri*. Is *this* where the Italians got their ideas from?) The mad doctor is helped in his endeavors by an old hag and her two sons (one a half-wit, the other a malicious dwarf). The dependable 1940s stereotypically crusading girl reporter (Luana Walters) is soon hot on his trail, after discovering that all of the brides

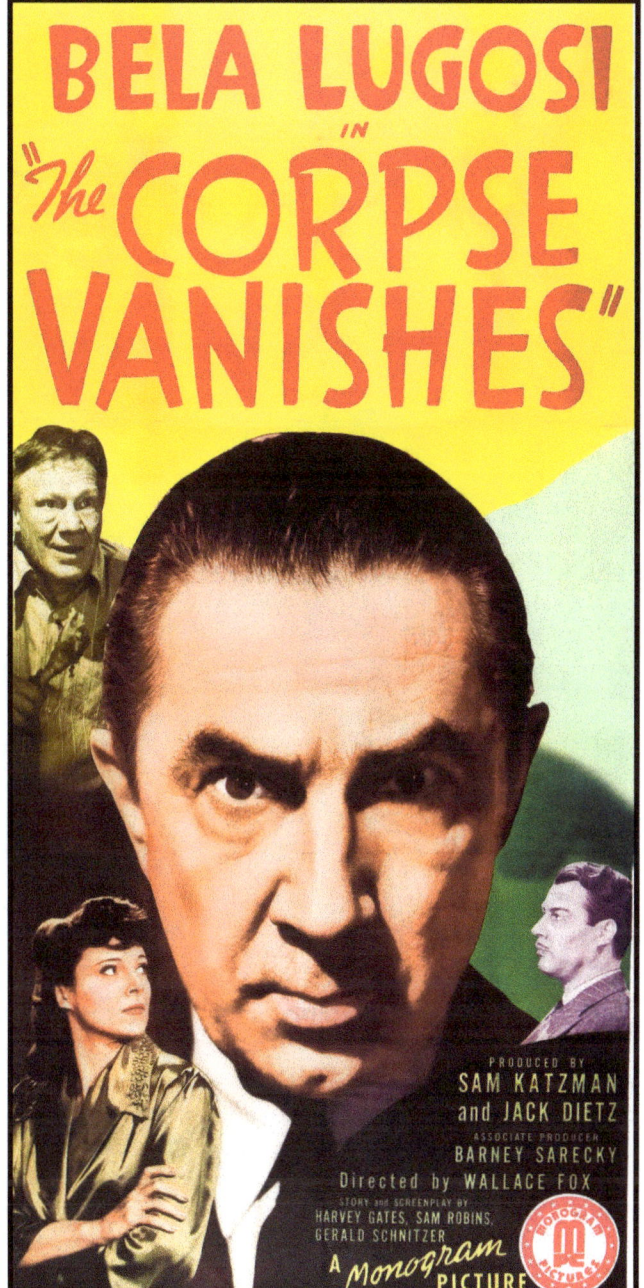

wore a rare, strange-smelling orchid on their wedding day and that Lugosi is the only person around who cultivates the flower. Could this orchid render the women unconscious to the point of near-death? Teaming up with a fellow doctor, the reporter worms her way into Lugosi's house on the pretext of an interview and eventually stumbles across the bodies of five brides kept in an underground vault. Sassy Walters then sets up a bogus wedding to trap the doctor, but sly Lugosi spots the set-up a mile off and kidnaps her instead. The usual frenetic climax ensues, with the dwarf and the dim-wit both killed, the old hag stabs Lugosi, Lugosi strangles the old hag before dying and his wife, deprived of the glandular fluid, rapidly ages and expires, while Walters escapes from the operating table in the nick of time. Taken at face value, this is fairly

any radioactivity in the area, as traces of radiation have been found near the murdered men, but Granger, in a ridiculous montage of stock footage, orders his eight killer zombies to blow-up vehicles, buildings and planes, as a warning to the police, also capturing Denning's best pal (bulky Karl Davis) and placing an atom brain in *his* head. You would think that when living corpse Davis visits Denning's house, Denning's wife and daughter would notice the ragged scar around their friend's head, not to mention his vacant expression and monosyllabic speech, but they don't. All Davis does is tear up the little girl's favorite doll and walk off. The ludicrous and (unintentionally) hilarious climax sees Granger killing scientist Gay, Davis bumping off Granger in revenge for his condition and blowing up the atomic laboratory; the always-lurching zombies attack the police *en masse* before expiring, as the lab is destroyed. This was *not* one of Columbia's cleverer efforts, even though it ran for years in the U.K., usually double billed with *The Werewolf* or *20 Million Miles to Earth*. Audiences were perhaps a little less discriminating in those days with their horror fare!

Barry Atkinson

The Curse of Frankenstein
Warner Bros., 1957; Director: Terence Fisher

Hammer's no-holds-barred foray into the world of Gothic horror cinema remains one of the most important genre movies ever made. Released in Britain to a storm of criticism from the critics, and upsetting the literary-minded set that couldn't believe (and *refused* to believe) the new-wave of British cinema would come up with something as downright nauseating as *this*. The first X-rated British horror movie in color proved to be an absolute sensation, delivering to post-war U.K. audiences used to a diet of Ealing comedies, Westerns, war movies and tame black-and-white thrillers, a severe shock. Hammer quickly fell foul of the censor's office that demanded in the future the company tone things down a bit (They didn't—[*Horror* of] *Dracula*, released a year later, was even more graphic in some instances); despite people fainting in their seats (particularly when Christopher Lee unwraps the bandages to reveal his gruesome, scarred features), the movie became a worldwide smash and Hammer was now a force to be reckoned with. This was very much a radical treatment of both Mary Shelley's original story and James Whale's 1931 *Frankenstein*. Peter Cushing (who had achieved some success in BBC-TV's 1954 adaptation of Orwell's *1984*) portrayed Baron Frankenstein as a well-mannered but cold-hearted achiever, showing little compassion for anyone or anything, including the luscious Hazel Court, as his fiancée Elizabeth, and his reluctant mentor-assistant, Robert Urquhart. His only aim in life was to create another being from body parts and corpses. Christopher Lee's Creature, buried under layers of makeup by Phil Leakey, resembled, in its black, high-collared jacket and contrasting chalk-white face, something out of a silent horror movie, but the actor's expert use of mime and

agreeable B fodder from the studio, with Lugosi putting a bit more effort into his "demented doctor" routine than usual, and as is the case with all of Monogram's horror features, the cacophonous musical score crashes merrily along in the background, boosting Lugosi's shadowy antics, becoming another bonus.

Barry Atkinson

Creature with the Atom Brain
Columbia, 1955; Director: Edward L. Cahn

Among Columbia's horror roster of the 1950s, Edward L. Cahn's combination of Nazis, gangsters, cops and atomic-powered zombies was an unattractive mix that didn't quite come off, and the normally reliable Cahn's direction was ponderous to say the least, lacking the director's customary flair. Mad scientist Gregory Gay, together with crime boss Michael Granger, is stealing bodies from the morgue and substituting the dead men's brains with atomic-engineered substitutes, sending off the super-strong zombies by remote control to kill members of Granger's old gang, who double-crossed him during a heist. The police, led by Richard Denning, organize cars and planes with sensors to search for

physical gestures (especially when Cushing orders him to stand up and sit down, while he is chained to a wall) brought this cadaverous figure to horrible life. Having the Creature shot in the face when he escapes into the woods only made his appearance more grotesque. Vivid EastmanColor photography, in beautiful rich green and mauves, complemented Cushing's sublime period laboratory. James Bernard's malevolent score, a menacing drone in the background, raised the goosebumps. A surfeit of dissections, bloody severed hands, eyeballs and brains popped up constantly to stun the public and raise the censor's wrath. Terence Fisher's impeccable and forceful direction took all of this in and raised the production to unheard levels of fright and tension. This seminal groundbreaker, together with 1958's *Dracula*, remains one of horror cinema's key works and was a major influence on directors in France, Italy and Spain, resulting in the so-called continental surgical/horror dramas such as Franco's *The Demon Doctor* and Franju's *Eyes Without a Face,* which proliferated after the release of Hammer's first and best-ever *Frankenstein* motion picture.

Barry Atkinson

Dead and Buried
Avco Embassy, 1981; Director: Gary Sherman

Now the horrible truth can be told…the 1980s were the worst decade in the history of the horror film. After a resurgence of gruesome independently produced American horrors and the proliferation of Euro Horror, the 1980s saw Hollywood creatively bankrupt and releasing rehashed imitations—copycat movies were the sad result.

Dead and Buried, script credited to Ronald Shuster and Dan O'Bannon, directed by Gary Sherman (*Raw Meat*), is an exception and remains one of the best independently produced horror movies of the 1980s.

First, what *Dead and Buried* does right is create an air of mystery and horror that draws the viewer immediately into the movie. We are confronted with the small rural town of Potter's Bluff (an allusion to *It's A Wonderful Life*'s alternate universe if mean Mr. Potter had controlled the town), a small community of seemingly friendly people, the type of town where everyone knows one another. In the film's first sequence a vacationing photographer meets a beautiful blonde on the beach, and in her naïve sexually charged way, she immediately starts to pose and even undress for him. Then purring, "Do you want me?" she begins to nuzzle close to the beaming man. Suddenly a crowd descends upon the poor sap, kicking and beating him over the head and finally wrapping him in fish net against a pole. "Welcome to Potter's Bluff," one man announces, pouring gasoline over him and setting him ablaze. The entire assembled crowd stands by smiling, watching him burn to death. This same scenario is repeated shortly thereafter with a drunken homeless person, who is harpooned and stabbed, as the wild-eyed mob snaps photos and giggles as the poor victim suffers and dies. This mob is visceral yet engaging.

Our titular hero, the town sheriff (James Farentino), a man who earned a master's degree in criminology but decided

to serve the needs of his home town, is mystified by these horrible, mutilating crimes. The beach victim, found at the wheel of an overturned auto accident, is burned to a crisp, yet his jaw drops and a chilling scream emulates from his throat. This victim is about to be questioned by the police, his head and body bandaged, when his nurse, the same seductive blonde from the beach, sticks a long hypodermic needle into his eye, killing him instantly. Strangely, days later the man is perfectly healed and working at the local service station.

The sheriff's investigation involves the local eccentric and nattily dressed town undertaker, Jack Albertson, who brags of his artistry and the fact that a closed coffin spells defeat for him. Albertson, always energetic and dancing to 1930s pop music as he works, seems to be disguising a sinister underbelly.

Soon the sheriff discovers his wife hiding a strange book on witchcraft and voodooism. Then a family of three stops at the town diner asking for directions, only to experience a car accident, which causes them to take refuge in an old house, one without electricity and covered with cobwebs (why then does the father venture alone down into the cellar with the happy wife yelling, is anyone home?). Shadows loom outside the windows. When our familiar town mob (now we begin to recognize that members of the murderous mob hold down

regular jobs in the community) breaks through the glass and attempts to murder the family, somehow they escape in a chilling visual sequence involving spooky, shadowy cinematography and well-executed editing. The next day their smashed car is pulled out of the river and the little boy turns up in a school classroom, just a quick flash to his classmates telegraphing the fact that this boy was apparently dead, but is now alive.

While the film's sense of dread and mystery is quite successful, the reliance on gore effects, created by the master Stan Winston no less, tend to go unnecessarily too far—with shots of rocks crushing skulls, people burned alive and victims getting needles in the eye rather excessive. [SPOILER ALERT] The film's final surprise, that this is a town of living corpses, people who died, reconstructed by masterful Jack Albertson and ultimately reanimated (although still dead and decaying) is a shocking one. In the film's final moments the sheriff learns via home movies that his wife murdered him while having sex—she stabbed repeatedly in the back. Looking now at his decaying fingers, the tender voice of Albertson states, let me fix that up, as the film ends on a freeze frame.

Dead and Buried succeeds on the strength of its quirky and well-executed performances (especially Jack Albertson's as the world's most kindly mad doctor) and its mystery-dominated horror plot that keeps the audience guessing right up until the ending. Stan Winston's makeup contributions are brilliant, especially a mortuary sequence where the smashed face of a teenage girl is restored to its original beauty, the final touch of adding an artificial eye to the socket a grisly coda. But instead of simply cutting away at this point, the girl's eyes open and she sits up and gets off the slab. Surprises like this abound, and the discrepancy between the Andy of Mayberry-style good people of Potter's Bluff and the insane mob of murderers that they sometimes become mesmerizes the audience and keeps it on its toes.

Gary J. Svehla

Dead Men Walk
PRC, 1943; Director: Sam Newfield

Independent company Producers Releasing Corporation were churning out their hoary old potboilers during the 1940s to keep the horror fans happy (and nearly all of their movies were X-rated in Britain), many starring the dour but solid George Zucco. With his clipped English enunciation, marble-like eyes and terse delivery of lines, Zucco always turned in a persuasive performance whatever he was appearing in and, in this one, the actor took on a kind of double act, a good-natured doctor and his vampiric twin brother; it was the only occasion that Zucco played a monster other than his usual mad doctor number. To add weight to an interesting little story, Dwight Frye was brought in to more or less reprise his *Dracula* role as the demented acolyte of the vampire twin. The picture opens with the evil brother being buried. Little do the mourners know that the local doctor pushed his brother off a cliff to his death, because the man was dabbling in demonology and ancient sorcery. But the evil twin has sworn revenge on his brother and rises from the dead as a vampire, killing one woman and vampirizing the doctor's niece (Mary Carlisle)—he wants her to accompany him into the realms of eternal night as one of the undead. A local woman, well-versed in superstitious folklore and convinced a vampire is at large, places a crucifix around Carlisle's neck, which wards off the bloodsucker on his next visit to her bedroom. Frye has to move the coffin to another crypt, when the doctor finally convinces Carlisle's dunderhead of a fiancé that his twin is the person responsible for Carlisle's condition. The ghostly vampire materializes before them, then fades away, and they go on a hunt for his burial place. The townsfolk storm Zucco's house in the final reel, mistakenly convinced *he* is the killer, but in the meantime the doctor has located his brother's tomb. In a struggle with the doctor, Frye gets crushed under an altar stone and the twins go up in flames when a falling candle sets fire to the building. The locals look on in horror as the timbers crash down on doctor and his twin, and the vampire's curse is lifted from Carlisle. Darkly photographed to underline the gloomy atmosphere, with Zucco excellent in both lead roles, *Dead Men Walk* is also far tighter in plot and action than PRC's other efforts from this period, and probably ranks as one of the actor's more gratifying horror flicks.

Barry Atkinson

Der Januskopf (Dr. Jekyll)
Lipow-Film, 1920; Director: F.W. Murnau

The further back one travels on the cinematic timeline, the more obscure the picture becomes. Such is the case with the missing horror film *Der Januskopf*, a 1920 German rendition of *Dr. Jekyll and Mr. Hyde*. The film's pedigree alone makes it a historically noteworthy effort, with direction by F.W. Murnau, scripting by Hans Janowitz, camerawork by Karl Freund and a showcase role for rising star Conrad Veidt (backed by Magnus Stifter, Margarete Schlegel and an up-and-coming supporting player named Bela Lugosi). Its plot also offered some novel twists on what would soon become an overly familiar tale. In this version, respectable Dr. O'Connor (Veidt) comes into the possession of a two-faced bust of the Roman god Janus, which begins to exert a strange effect on his personality. Transformed into Mr. Warren, his monstrous alter ego, he resorts to sundry crimes, including the murder of a small child and the abduction of heroine Schlegel. Unable to free himself from the statue's pernicious influence, O'Connor swallows a vial of poison, dying with the accursed figure clutched in his hands.

Along with *The Cabinet of Dr. Caligari* and *Der Mude Tod*, *Der Januskopf* was an early example of German Expressionism, the film school that would later exert a prime influence on the Universal horror classics of the 1930s. Existing stills confirm that the film was infused with the relentless sense of paranoia and arty, atmospheric visuals that distinguish the European Expressionist horrors from their more prosaic American counterparts. (Theoretical comparisons to the John Barrymore *Dr. Jekyll and Mr. Hyde*, released that same year, are particularly intriguing.) A quick look at these stills leads one to imagine how the film's theme of dual identity was made even more compelling via the subtext of dark fate, a hallmark of the early German cinema. Extant reviews are interesting also, such as Berlin's *Film-Kurier* (April 29, 1920), which notes, "One feels tense and taunt, even when one knows in advance how the plot will proceed," and that Veidt "speaks…with his body, with his hands…he carries off the role, fulfills it perhaps as no other German actor could." Another factor in the film's favor was the reputation of director Murnau, a gifted filmmaker who would later helm such critically esteemed features as *The Last Laugh, Sunrise* and the legendary *Nosferatu*, universally regarded as one of the silent screen's greatest horror films.

Various hypotheses have been offered to explain *Der Januskopf*'s disappearance, none of them entirely satisfactory. Some researchers contend that the problem stemmed from the unauthorized adaptation of the source material. The re-christening of the film's main character has, in fact, been widely interpreted as an acknowledgment that a copyright infringement issue did exist. According to this theory, a civil lawsuit was threatened by the Stevenson estate, prompting production company Delca-Bioscop to destroy all known copies of the movie as part of an out-of-court settlement. But John Soister, a recent researcher on the filmography of Conrad Veidt, is aware of no documentation that supports this thesis. In addition, he finds it questionable that Murnau would have been allowed to adopt a similarly risky strategy on *Nosferatu* a mere two years after having been burned on *Der Januskopf*. In either case, the film is said to have had distribution under the alternate titles *The Head of Janus* and *Love's Mockery*, although the Library of Congress is unable to provide confirmation of a U.S. release. All that remains today is the film's script and a handful of stills, originally housed at the Swedish Film Archives.

Steven Thornton

The Devil Commands
Columbia, 1941; Director Edward Dmytryk

Back in 1941, Boris Karloff was about to conclude what has come to be known as his four Columbia Mad Doctor pictures; the best remains *The Devil Commands*. Director Edward Dmytryk, soon to leave B programmers behind, was on the brink of an outstanding motion picture career (*The Caine Mutiny, Murder My Sweet, Raintree County*). So we have Boris Karloff in a performance that is both sympathetic and monstrous (and he's on screen in almost every sequence), working with a first-rate director in a tight 65-minute B production that thoroughly entertains.

The film opens in noirish voiceover fashion, and ends the same way, with a moody shot of a spooky old home out in the

country. Karloff begins the movie with slicked-to-the-side dark hair, portraying a respected science department chair of the local college whose research (communication using thought projection and brainwaves) upsets his university peers. In a gut-wrenching sequence, Karloff's wife dies tragically in a car accident, Karloff's spirit dying with her. Now his research turns to contacting the dead, and after hooking up with a fake spiritualist, a very domineering woman Mrs. Walters (Anne Revere in one of the strongest female horror film performances of the 1940s), he ignores his grieving daughter and surfaces two years later, now with dour expression and graying hair that is demonically frizzy and wild. His laboratory is unlike any lab in horror film history, with corpses seated around a table with metal helmets around their heads, which, when activated, create a whirlwind of tornado activity causing the stiffs to lean inward toward the center of the table. For a low budget picture, such special effects aided immeasurably, for the storm-within-the-lab sounds are quite effective.

Interestingly, Boris Karloff's performance runs the gamut of emotions, from dutiful father and husband to obsessive scientist, grieving widower, pathetic victim and emotionally vacant automaton. For a B production, Karloff dares to convey the heightened emotions that Bela Lugosi always gets credit for creating in his B movies made during the same time. It is definitely one of Karloff's finest 1940s performances, and the film more than holds up its end (its sometimes too abrupt ending only channels the theme that humans that invade God's turf are doomed to sudden destruction).

Gary J. Svehla

Doctor Blood's Coffin
United Artists 1960; Director: Sidney J. Furie

This lively British horror outing features Kieron Moore as a young doctor returning to his father's medical practice in the far west of Cornwall. He takes up illegal heart surgery in the village and administers to his unwilling victims a potion originating from the Orinoco in South America. This places them in a state of catalepsy that enables the doctor to carry out his experiments, which take place in underground tunnels in abandoned mines, where he sets up his laboratory. The death toll mounts in the small Cornish village after one botched open-heart operation after another. Moore declares his undying love and medical ambitions to Britain's reigning Queen of Horror, delicious Hazel Court (his father's assistant), by digging up the rotting body of her dead husband and giving it a new heart. Couldn't he have shown his devotion to her, or his medical expertise, less dramatically? As a result, the reactivated decaying corpse strangles Moore as Court escapes through the mine passages to safety on the beach, as the police close in. Moore, an up-and-coming actor when the film was made, gave an edgy, overwrought performance as the distinctly unethical doctor hell-bent on proving his theories no matter who suffered in the process, and director Sidney Furie made good location use of the derelict tin and copper mines

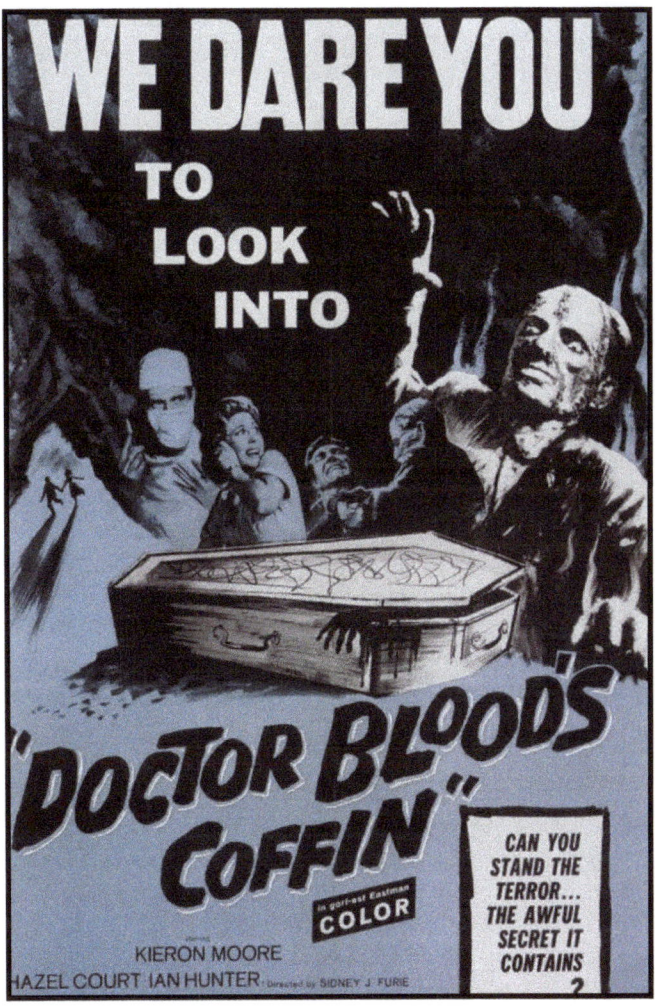

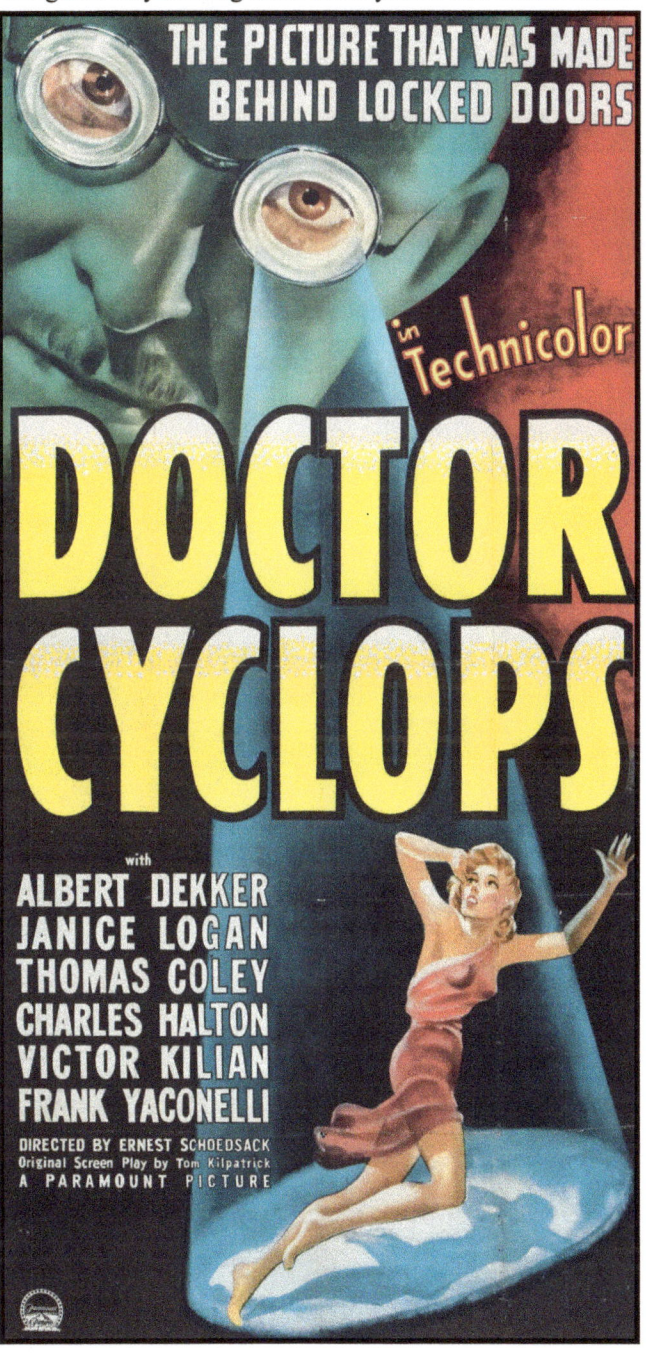

that litter this part of the bleak coastline in Cornwall, making an unusual backdrop for Moore's nefarious activities. This was typical British horror fare of its day, cruder and rougher around the edges than the more superior Hammer movies of the same period, but just as colorful and engaging, filmed at breakneck speed by Furie.

Barry Atkinson

Dr. Cyclops
Paramount, 1940; Director: Ernest B. Schoedsack

Dr. Cyclops is the anomaly, a Universal monster/adventure epic released in 1940 in beautiful Technicolor photography. Directed by Ernest B. Schoedsack, the man who directed *King Kong*, *Dr. Cyclops* plays more as an adventure film with a featured mad scientist, who creates miniature human victims, than as an all-out horror or even science fiction movie. However, I feel *Dr. Cyclops* shares roots with a classic Universal horror movie, *The Invisible Ray* (1936). Instead of having the reclusive madman Janos (Boris Karloff), we have the equally myoptic Dr. Thorkel (Albert Dekker), whose soda-bottle lenses become his downfall (both symbolically and literally). Each scientist finds the source of his power and scientific discovery at the bottom of a tunnel drilled into the Earth. The radiation found could be a source of great good or great evil, and each deluded scientist uses his discovery for evil.

Both Janos and Dr. Thorkel share basic character traits. Thorkel invites a team of great scientific minds to the jungles of Peru, they think they are to join his team. Since Thorkel works alone, this is a major breakthrough. However, once the scientists arrive and are praised to high heaven by Thorkel, he invites them to look through his microscope and confirm his findings (his deteriorating eyesight does not allow him to see clearly through the microscope). He then unceremoniously invites them to leave for home tomorrow morning, his arrogance only needing those extra eyes for one brief moment.

No longer valued, the scientific team is almost kicked out of camp. Janos, also a loner and recluse and a man who does not work well with other people, according to his blind mother, finds his own discovery taken from him by the scientific team that assumes too much power. So in both films we get a ying and yang effect of the balancing act between maverick, loner scientist and a more scientifically approved team—and how the two should work together.

But the fun of *Dr. Cyclops* is watching the dedicated team of scientists reduced to doll size and survive against the god-like captivity that Thorkel imposes upon them. Of course the goal of the little people is to take Thorkel's glasses and render the god blind, a raving Cyclops so to speak, and then use their intelligence to take him down. These sequences show the cleverness of man taming his environment, and such conflict creates the adventure that the film is best known for. It is in these action sequences that director Schoedsack shines. And the Technicolor photography becomes an impressive technical gimmick back in 1940. The film's allusions to mythology (even Thorkel's name, when shortened to Thor, illustrates his god-like status) add another level of meaning that only makes the film richer. Albert Dekker's performance as the calm, arrogant giant of a mad scientist still impresses today.

Gary J. Svehla

Dr. Jekyll and Mr. Hyde
Paramount, 1931; Director: Rouben Mamoulian
Dr. Jekyll and Mr. Hyde
MGM, 1941; Director: Victor Fleming

The Rouben Mamoulian-directed version of *Dr. Jekyll and Mr. Hyde* that stars Fredric March (who was co-winner for Best Actor at the Academy Awards for his performance as Jekyll and Hyde) is perhaps the greatest non-Universal horror classic of the 1930s. Even though sound cinema was still in its infancy, Mamoulian amplifies every grasp as Jekyll transforms into monstrous Hyde, emphasizes every bubbling beaker in his laboratory and sometimes allows the sound of a broken cane smashing the human skull to depict grisly murders graphically. Mamoulian starts off his innovative movie with a subjective sequence allowing the movie audience to become Jekyll, the audience seeing its own face when the good doctor glances into a mirror. Later, when Jekyll first transforms into Hyde, the audience watches the sequence subjectively, with our own hands mixing chemicals and gulping them down.

What makes this version of Jekyll and Hyde a classic horror movie is the fact that Hyde is a primitive, simian version of earlier man, stripped of his social consciousness, allowing the beast to dominate. Basically, the movie is a wereape tale where a decent human being transforms into his primordial pre-civilized self, first induced by chemicals, but soon induced by the simple power of mind over matter, as the beast gains control over the rational human.

March as Hyde is breathtaking in a landmark performance that still rivets audiences today. When the apeman Hyde,

wearing top hat and tails, goes into the rainy evening, looking skyward and opening his mouth to taste the rain, such a simple sequence sums up all our primitive pleasures. In the club sequence with Ivy (Miriam Hopkins), where Hyde attempts to woo her with his bottle of champagne and promise of money to be thrown her way, the sexually driven man, whose self-imposed sense of power fuels his libido, becomes classic cinema. Contrasted is the earlier sequence where the not-so-innocent Jekyll comes to Ivy's aide, taking her home and putting her in bed. There she playfully strips for the good doctor, plants kisses on his lips and dangles her naked leg from underneath her flimsy covers and moans, "Come back soon!" Best friend Lanyon (Holmes Herbert) interrupts his friend Jekyll, who is interested physically in the sex kitten, but Lanyon reminds Jekyll of his decency and social consciousness. However, the doctor's sexual longing for the desirable lower-class tart surface in the guise of Mr. Hyde.

Rose Hobart is unfortunately bland (perhaps emoting her performance in a decidedly non-sexual manner to contrast herself against the sexually oozing Ivy) as good-girl Muriel Carew, Jekyll's fiancée. The polite young thing is bound by the dictates of her oppressive society, as represented by her father. Equally bland and stiff is Fredric March as Jekyll, who delivers lines such as "This is my penance," which he announces to God, looking skyward, promising he will give up the love of his life in order to maintain his humanity. Whereas as Hyde, March exudes delirious energy in a performance that literally twitches. By contrast Jekyll's every line seems overly rehearsed, deliberate and theatrical. But March's Hyde

version Spencer Tracy portrays the dual roles with luscious cinematic sex symbols Ingrid Bergman (as Ivy) and Lana Turner (fiancée Beatrix) as the female sex/love interest. In this Victor Fleming-directed production, Bergman and Turner are interestingly cast against type, with Bergman playing the lower-class floozy, who attempts to seduce the good doctor, and usual femme fatale Turner playing the socially acceptable demure bride-to-be of Jekyll. While Mamoulian's movie was cast as hardcore horror with the emphasis on Jekyll's transformation into the simian Hyde, 10 years later the Fleming version seems more Hollywood mainstream and focuses on Freudian suspense and romance (let's face it, Miriam Hopkins was sexual from the neck down but she was no classic beauty), courtesy of Turner and Bergman, two of Hollywood's sizzling female stars of the era. The movie's most innovative sequences involve brief Freudian dream/visions as Jekyll transforms into Hyde. Sequences of the two females smiling seductively, overtly tempting the socially acceptable Jekyll into sexual merriment, is best symbolized by the sequence of Jekyll gleefully riding a white horse and fiercely whipping the poor beast to run faster, a delirious look on Hyde's face. When suddenly, in the dream, the horse morphs into the naked shoulders and head of Bergman and Turner. While such dream sequences are short, they are visually tantalizing and symbolic of the raging desires bubbling just below Jekyll's surface (or stirring just below the waist).

Spencer Tracy's Dr. Jekyll, becoming a more complex character than March was ever allowed to be back in 1931, is passionate about medical science being a business of risk taking and self-sacrifice, and gallantly he decides to put his life on the line to advance knowledge. Tracy, squat and not conventionally handsome (at least when compared to March), becomes a figure of passion and commitment. However, his Edward Hyde is subtle and almost ordinary looking. Just as March's Hyde progressively deteriorated and became uglier with each transformation, Tracy's initial transformations make him look different, perhaps bed-headed and wild-eyed, but definitely not monstrous. Even at the end of the movie, his Hyde develops bags beneath his eyes, his eyebrows grow wild and bushy and his hair becomes messy, but no one would mistake him for a gorilla in top hat and tails. While audiences wish for Tracy's Hyde to become monstrous and bestial, his transformation is one of internal characterization based more upon acting than makeup. While both approaches are valid, I prefer March's monster over Tracy's human degenerate approach for Hyde. So while March earns my attention for his classic Hyde performance, Tracy wins me over with his multi-layered and superior performance as Jekyll.

Gary J. Svehla

joins the ranks of iconic horror film performances and every sequence in which Hyde appears is a classic one.

This Mamoulian 1931 Paramount gem almost disappeared when MGM decided to remake the Paramount version 10 years later. Hoping to avoid comparisons between the two productions, MGM attempted to buy the rights to the earlier production, so they could destroy prints and make their own version of *Dr. Jekyll and Mr. Hyde* the definitive one. In this

Dr. Orloff's Monster
AIP-TV, 1964; Director: Jesus Franco

Director Jesus/Jess Franco was off to a promising start with *The Awful Dr. Orlof*, produced in 1962 and released to

America two years later. The intense Howard Vernon created a stellar villain, a mad scientist obsessed with restoring beauty to his disfigured daughter. Franco, both as screenwriter and director, created an ominous Gothic mood, featuring a terrifying monster. A sequel only promised to be better!

However, the direct sequel to *The Awful Dr. Orlof* was released in 1964 and was called *Dr. Orloff's Monster* in America, but released in France as *The Brides of Dr. Jekyll* (the sub-titled print available from Image goes by this title). So the titular Orloff is not really Orloff at all, but he really isn't Dr. Jekyll either...he's a low-key Dr. Fisherman (Marcelo Arroita-Jauregui, looking similar to Pierre Brasseur's evil Dr. Genessier from *Eyes Without a Face*, the French horror classic). Thus, Fisherman, a disciple of Orloff's, only makes us wish that Howard Vernon had returned to repeat his performance.

Wisely, Franco maintains the dank, black-and-white mood of the original, but sometimes the moody photography only reminds the audience that *Dr. Orloff's Monster* is all style, without the benefit of an involving story. Franco does attempt to imbue the movie with pathos and sympathy, but the lack of consistent acting talent and gratuitous nudity sinks the production. Basically, the story follows Melissa, a young woman, as she spends her Christmas vacation at the home of her aunt and uncle (the aunt buries herself in the bottle, while her uncle hides in his private laboratory). It turns out that Melissa's father, a man she never knew, had an affair with her aunt and her uncle murdered him. Now the mad Fisherman taunts the corpse of his brother, by transforming him into a murderous automaton, commanded to kill strippers via electronic signals emitted from necklaces Fisherman givesto the women beforehand. Most of the self-conscious strippers unflatteringly disrobe for the camera—revealing not their charms, but their physical inadequacies in long, protracted striptease sequences. The murders themselves are too soon telegraphed, becoming unspectacular and dreary. Far too much time is wasted in underlit jazz clubs, where musical interludes become obvious space-fillers.

Only near the movie's end, when Melissa becomes aware of her father's reanimation as a zombie, does Franco attempt to create an emotional connection that transcends the ridiculous.But it is too little too late and only reinforces the missed potential of what this movie might have become. After the promise of *The Awful Dr. Orlof*, *Dr. Orloff's Monster* only foreshadows the declining creative powers Jess Franco would demonstrate in his future work.

Gary J. Svehla

Doctor X
First National, 1932; Director: Michael Curtiz

[Author Steven Thornton imaged *Doctor X*, an early sound film, as an example of the tremendous creative leaps and bounds sound brought to classic horror cinema. In his review, he imagines what the movie might have been like if silent cinema lingered a while longer, and how effectively director Michael Curtiz used sound technology to make this classic film even better.]

This Michael Curtiz-directed thriller incorporated sound so deftly that to imagine the film as a silent is to rethink the work in its entirety.

Ambient noise and throwaway dialogue is used so freely in *Dr. X* that one scarcely notices it. Such touches as the moan of the Cape Cod wind, the clatter of autopsy instruments and the jolt of Lee Tracy's joy buzzer do much to keep the audience on the edge of its seat. This effect adds to the pace as well, especially in the chaotic aftermath of the sequences in which the "moon killer" murders are restaged. Dialogue, hammered out with the cadence of a typewriter, also enhances the mood of the film. Supporting characters benefit from this greatly; the personalities of beat cops, ladies of the night and house servants virtually come alive through the use of the spoken word. And note the unsavory voices of Xavier's scientific colleagues. In a silent world, this effect could only have been approximated through the use of visual stereotypes suggesting foreign (and presumably undesirable) origin.

Sound also adds a dimension to the performances of the film's lead players. Atwill's clipped diction quickly establishes him as the film's first red herring, while Lee Tracy's nervous prattle and Fay Wray's sexy aloofness generate romantic sparks in abundance. Hearing this trio, one can easily identify the aural signature that was fast becoming a First National/Warner Bros. trademark. It should also be noted how the film's dialogue conveys a comic yet macabre undercurrent. Any attempt to capture this "whistling in the dark" quality via the use of title cards would likely stun viewers, just like hitting them over the head with the *subtlety* of a sledge hammer.

Dr. X does provide some memorable visual touches and it is these that a silent version would have to more fully explore. A persistent use of shadows paints the sets in dark, menacing imagery. Odd angles and intense close-ups fill the screen, rendering the viewer slightly off kilter. Other visual cues boarder on the comic, such as the bouncing skeletons or the "John Doe" tag attached to Lee Tracy's foot as he hides in the morgue. The weird ambiance of the early two-color process, with its emphasis on red-green, also contributes to an otherworldly look. Once underway, the story settles into "old

dark house" mode, a tradition that had a long and venerable history in the silent cinema. Without the transforming element of sound, this film's kinship with *The Bat* and *The Cat and the Canary* would likely be much more apparent.

The initial wave of sound films relied on the flawless elocution of actors who had extensive training in the theater. Before long, however, a new style of performing had evolved, one that drew its inspiration from the rhythms and speech patterns of the everyday life. *Dr. X* takes full advantage of this shift, using it to pull us into the film and persuading us to turn a blind eye to the implausible nature of the plot. Sans sound, our willingness to suspend disbelief would have been stretched to the breaking point, a problem that bedevils many horror efforts of the silent era. For *Dr. X*, consequently, sound is an indispensable component, essential in ways that other Golden Age horrors did not require.

Steven Thornton

Evil of Frankenstein
Universal, 1964; Director: Freddie Francis

Terence Fisher, ignored by Hammer because of his perceived failure with *The Phantom of the Opera*, was overlooked for their third *Frankenstein* picture, Freddie Francis instead took up the director's reins. *The Evil of Frankenstein* is one of Hammer's most underrated horror (and *Frankenstein*) flicks, and it's hard to understand why, particularly when you compare it to the three that came after, the uninteresting *Frankenstein Created Woman*, the unappetizing *Frankenstein Must Be Destroyed* (both directed by Fisher) and the abysmal *The Horror of Frankenstein*. All of Hammer's renowned quality trademarks are set firmly in place: Peter Cushing again excelling as the Baron; lush color; fine period sets; a ruinous Gothic castle; a marvelous laboratory (one of Hammer's best); a more contemporary score by Don Banks and a decent monster, played by Kiwi Kingston. Having procured the rights from Universal to their original horror output, Universal allowed the company to incorporate some of Jack Pierce's ideas for the monster makeup, and Kingston does resemble slightly the old Boris Karloff monster, although rougher and less refined, sporting a distinct square head, tatty sackcloth suit and heavy boots. In flashback, we see Cushing create Kingston in his lab, teaching him how to eat and drink. Francis uses a tremendous subjective shot here, as Kingston, foreground but out of focus, eyes Cushing menacingly, the Baron hesitantly edging towards him with a tray full of food. Chased out of his castle by the police, Cushing is imprisoned but escapes, while the monster, pursued by the villagers, falls from a cliff into a glacier. Years later, the Baron returns to Karlstadt with young assistant Sandor Eles, taking up residence in his empty,

pictures, considering the director preferred the widescreen format prevalent in all his other works.

Barry Atkinson

Eyes Without A Face
Lopert, 1960; Director: Georges Franju

Many of us first encountered *Eyes Without a Face* in its butchered American re-edited version, 1963's *The Horror Chamber of Dr. Faustus*, the other half of the double-bill with *The Manster*. But that bastardized version is nothing like seeing the original French Georges Franju version. The movie's stark black-and-white photography by Eugen Schufftan (aka Shuftan) is among the eeriest ever concocted for a horror film classic, showcasing naked corpses in trenchcoats being dumped into a river, dank kennels with caged raging dogs, the no-frills operating room, the cold police station, the darkly lit morgue and the gloomy mausoleum, each establishing set pieces of morbid and depressed horror. *Eyes Without a Face* is not a black and white movie; it is best described as black and gray.

The three performances that tantalize are the wonderful Pierre Brasseur as Dr. Genessier, Alida Valli as his assistant Louise and Edith Scob as Genessier's daughter, Christiane. Brasseur is perhaps the horror genre's most unique mad doctor, simply because he underplays the role to absolute perfection. His frozen face and hollow eyes are sublime when he is called to the morgue and asked to identify his daughter, which he does (even though the corpse belongs to that of his victim, *not* his own daughter). And when the actual father of the victim with tear-filled eyes pleads with Genessier to confirm the corpse was the doctor's daughter, Genessier coldly accuses the desperate man of trying to squeeze comfort from him, when it is his own daughter who is dead, cold on the slab. Such an icy demeanor only accentuates the internal evil this doctor projects, a doctor who is sacrificing young victims to attempt to restore his daughter's ravished face, a face destroyed in an auto accident caused by Genessier himself. Creating a counterpart to the over-the-top mad doc played by a Colin Clive or a Bela Lugosi, Pierre Brasseur is always coolly calculating, all his rage and pain is internal, silently held in check. It's a masterful performance.

Alida Valli, soon to be known for her appearances in Italian horror movies, is interesting in an almost silent role as the assistant (her face also reconstructed…a scar on her neck hidden by necklaces) to Genessier (it is always apparent she loves the doctor). She waits unseen in cars on crowded Paris streets, attempting to find the right young girl with the proper facial features to become the latest medical guinea pig. In other sequences, she becomes almost like a mother to the disturbed Christiane, comforting the girl and giving her hope that her father will be able to restore her face. Valli's is a supporting role, but it is one that lingers.

However, perhaps the most interesting performance is that of Edith Scob as the hauntingly beautiful Christiane,

leaf-strewn chateau and, with the aid of a deaf-mute village girl (Katy Wild), discovers his monster perfectly preserved in the glacier ice. Thawed out from its icy tomb (copied scene-for-scene from 1944's *House of Frankenstein,* where Karloff thaws out the Frankenstein monster and the Wolf Man), Kingston is reactivated, but the brain doesn't function. A dodgy hypnotist (oily Peter Woodthorpe), on the run from creditors, is asked by Cushing to unlock the creature's mind, which he succeeds in doing, but then Woodthorpe controls the creature himself for his own vengeful ends, instructing the lumbering brute to fetch him gold from the village and murder the local burgomaster and chief of police. Killing the burgomaster and a constable, the creature (cared for by Wild) gets drunk on brandy, shoves a metal spike into Woodthorpe and wrecks Cushing's laboratory—the Baron and his creation go up in flames as the castle blows sky-high, leaving Eles and Wild to run for safety. Much grittier and harder-edged than other Hammer fodder from this period, Cushing's Frankenstein is almost heroic in comparison to the loathsome Woodthorpe and the blundering chief of police (Duncan Lemont), sacrificing himself in the fiery climax so that the two youngsters can get free of the castle, a performance more sympathetic than his other five in the role of the Baron. Along with *The Brides of Dracula* and *The Mummy, The Evil of Frankenstein* was a big hit in many countries for a number of years, one of Hammer's most popular exports, and also one of Freddie Francis' classier the girl who wears an ivory face mask that only reveals her hair and eyes, making her face as rigid yet as beautiful as any statue crafted by any Italian artist. Christiane is often viewed curled up in a fetal position on the couch. Her wide, sad eyes are a mirror to her soul, revealing a young woman lost in hopelessness. Even after her face is restored and the mask is gone, her actual facial features do not appear much different than when she was wearing the mask, but her short-term hope is lost as her face slowly deteriorates, captured in a series of still photographs shot over the course of almost one week. Earlier, from a subjective focus, the audience caught a blurred shot of Christiane's mask-less face, as she stared at the face of the victim-to-be lying helpless on the operating table. Christiane's depression is caused by the fact that even if the operation is successful, her success means the disfigurement or even death of an innocent girl, much like herself. At the movie's climax she releases the wild dogs, feral beasts that maul the face of the unsuspecting Dr. Genessier. She also sets free the doves, whose white poetic presence in the dark night serves more as an image of beauty on which to end the film. In the literal sense, the film offers no dramatic resolution. *Eyes Without a Face* ends on such a note of quiet, intense beauty, allowing such imagery to create its own conclusion.

Gary J. Svehla

The Fly
20th Century Fox, 1958; Director: Kurt Neumann

The unexpected success of *The Fly* took Fox completely by surprise, compensating for losses incurred in other more expensive productions around that period; without doubt, a horror film in CinemaScope *and* color was a major factor in pulling-power, as was Vincent Price, although on this occasion, the actor was on the side of good for a change. Opening with the gruesome sight of a blood-spattered hydraulic press, the story unfolds in flashback. Patricia Owens is arrested for the bizarre murder of her husband and relates, to brother-in-law Price and police inspector Herbert Marshall, the events leading up to his death. After a slow 30-minute build up, the action steps up a notch. Al "David" Hedison plays a scientist experimenting with the transfer of matter through a disintegrator-integrator machine, mystified when a plate he sends through the transmitter re-emerges with the makers' name in reverse. His pet cat also disappears into the ether. Perfecting his techniques, he successfully transmits a guinea pig without letting on to Owens that he himself will be the next subject to enter the machine. Routinely paced to begin with, featuring a splendid Gothic-like laboratory, Hedison transports himself as the audience is left to ponder two things—why are Owens and her son trying to locate a strange-looking fly with a white head and arm, and what has caused Hedison to lock his laboratory door, passing notes underneath to his bewildered wife? The truth is revealed when Owens, allowed to enter the lab to give her husband a bowl of milk laced with rum, sees him walking around with a black sheet over his head, his left arm tucked inside his coat; the coat, for a second, falls, exposing Hedison's fly arm. A fly entered the transmitter during the experiment and the scientist now sports the head and arm of a blowfly. The moment Owens unmasks Hedison is as startling as the unmasking scene in *House of Wax*. Entering the transmitting machine at his wife's request, she opens the door to the second machine, hoping that the transfer has worked, restoring her husband to his former self. Emerging from the machine, Owens clasps Hedison by his shoulders and removes the covering, screaming in terror as the fly's face stares back, its mouth quivering. On the big screen, this sequence created quite a stir in its day. Owens' features are seen from the fly's perspective, multifaceted images that represent one of sci-fi's more novel moments of shock. As the fly's genetics slowly impinge on the scientist's thought processes, he begins to deteriorate mentally (an effective bit of acting from Hedison in these scenes), his fly arm acting savagely, almost in opposition to his human side (as when he caresses the unconscious Owens, his fly persona hovering murderously over his wife, only to be forced aside by Hedison's rapidly dwindling human emotions). Unable to locate the blowfly that will restore her husband, the almost deranged scientist pathetically (but movingly) scrawls "I Love You" on his blackboard before pleading with Owens to end his life, which she does, crushing his head and mutated arm under a hydraulic press. The infamous climax, where the Hedison fly is trapped on a spider's web screeching "Help me! Help me!" before Marshall crushes it and the spider with a rock, is cinematic kitsch at its most outlandish, but it works beautifully and Owens, in the final reel, is let off the hook legally. Regrettably, Neumann died shortly after completing the picture so was never able to take the credit for coming up with one of the 1950s most memorable, money-spinning horror movies that spawned two sequels, 1959's *Return of the Fly* (excellent),1965's *Curse of the Fly* (inferior) and David Cronenberg's grisly remake in 1986.

Barry Atkinson

The Fly
20th Century Fox, 1986; Director: David Cronenberg

This may be Cronenberg's most intimate horror film to date. Only three main characters are involved and most of the picture's action takes place in Jeff Goldblum's workshop, set inside a cavernous, disused warehouse. Physicist Seth Brundle (Goldblum) has invented a teleportation machine, but is experiencing problems with transporting live tissue. Journalist Geena Davis decides to take up his offer to make his experiment her pet project, which will culminate in Goldblum teleporting himself from one machine to another. Geena falls for the goofy, self-effacing physicist (mirroring their real, off-screen romance), causing her oily boss/ex-lover John Getz to pester her for sexual favors, being in a perpetual state of jealousy. The "eternal triangle" aspect, and a pretty unemotional one at that, plays alongside Goldblum's own feelings for Davis; piqued by her on/off relationship with the smarmy Getz, he transports himself prematurely, but a fly ends up in the telepod with him and their genes become fused. But this is not like Fox's 1958 version when David Hedison emerged with a giant fly's head. Goldblum at first possesses the increased strength of an athlete with unlimited sexual desire and a craving for sugar, before his body gradually begins its slow transformation into something more terrible than he could ever have imagined. It is now that Cronenberg piles on the stomach-churning effects, as Goldblum begins to lose body parts (teeth and nails at first), his blotchy, leprous skin covered in muck as he unceremoniously vomits in front of a horrified Davis. These graphically sick scenes are offset by Goldblum's philosophical, semi-humorous approach to his condition: "I'd like to become the first insect politician" he tells Davis, while referring to himself as "Brundle-fly," and all his rejected body parts are kept in a cabinet to remind himself of what he used to be. The moment when Davis, pregnant by the physicist, decides to leave him to his fate is heart-rending, the by-now grotesque Goldblum sobbing and hitting his misshapen head in despair; minutes later, he espies from the roof of the warehouse Davis and Getz driving off together, much like Quasimodo looking down at the crowds from the ramparts of Notre Dame cathedral. The inclusion of a dream sequence, in which Davis gives birth to a giant maggot, is perhaps a step too far, given the amount of gore on display; as she is about to have an abortion, the deformed Goldblum crashes through a window into the surgery and carries her off to his abode. Cronenberg cranks up the tension, and the revolting images, in the climax, as Getz enters the workshop furtively with a loaded shotgun, when a shadow flits across the ceiling; it's Goldblum, who leaps down and spews corrosive acid over Getz's left hand and leg. Grabbing Davis, Goldblum's intentions are to merge himself, her and the unborn child in one pod to create "the perfect family." The terrified woman batters away at his face, completing the metamorphosis; shedding its outer flesh, the fly-monster has emerged. Finally, after Davis escapes from the pod, Goldblum is transformed one last time into a malformed, twisted mutation before Davis, at the almost incoherent pleas

Leslie Neilsen and crew look over the beautiful Alta (Anne Francis) and father Morbius (Walter Pidgeon), from *Forbidden Planet*.

of the creature, blasts it to death with Getz's gun. Goldblum was Oscar-nominated for his role as the gawky scientist in an intelligent, carefully structured but pretty gross reworking of the 1958 kitsch classic that, over 20 years on, still needs to be viewed on an empty stomach.

Barry Atkinson

Forbidden Planet
MGM, 1956; Director: Fred M. Wilcox

When it comes to classic science fiction cinema, MGM's *Forbidden Planet* is a landmark film, with its CinemaScope and color planetscape photography and special effects-created planet, Altair 4. Besides the outstanding cast that includes the never lovelier Anne Francis, Walter Pidgeon, Leslie Neilsen, Jack Kelly and Robby the Robot, the film features Walter Pidgeon as Dr. Morbius, one of the more unique mad scientists in film history. The all-powerful Morbius, who lives on heavenly planet Altair-4 with his lovely daughter Alta (Anne Francis), are the only living survivors of a colonization party that inhabited the planet for 20 years. When the rescue/investigation rocket lands, headed by Commander Adams (Nielsen), to assist the survivors, Morbius, outwardly polite, makes it apparent the crew of young men are unnecessary and distracting to his scientific work. In other words, he wants them gone as soon as possible. Part of the problem is his over-protectiveness of his innocent, virgin daughter, metaphorically fully ripe on the vine and ready for picking. And with all these lusty military males, who clean up pretty well in their spiffy uniforms, are very interested in chatting up Alta. However, Morbius is not impressed.

Dr. Morbius has a shrewdly inquisitive mind and has spent the past decades investigating the advanced technology of the now dead race, the Krells, who once populated the planet. These masterminds have so much knowledge to offer the less sophisticated Earthlings, and Morbius knows that even in his limited remaining years he will never absorb all the technology of their advanced super science.

It soon becomes apparent to the visiting space crew that some mysterious energy force is roaming the planet and committing acts of mass destruction, hampering the efforts of the crew to solve the mystery of the disappearance of the former colony members. Just by thinking, Morbius has mastered the Krell technology that allows his mind to create an all powerful thought monster that can do his bidding. Even worse is the fact that Morbius' subconscious thoughts (that he is not consciously thinking), can also activate this monster from his Freudian Id. Perhaps it is a father's concern over the budding sexuality of his daughter and his obsessive desire to protect her from her own natural desires, or perhaps subconsciously Morbius maintains incestual desires toward his own sex-kitten daughter, but the Id monster's attacks become more frequent and more brutal, and by the film's end this psychic energy builds to massively destructive proportions when Morbius understands, just as the Krell understood, that this powerful technology is simply too strong to harness. In the best sense of self-sacrifice and because of his love for Alta, Morbius directs the power of his own Id against himself, destroying

An original lobby card frm *Frankenstein* (1931), featuring Colin Clive as Dr. Frankenstein at far right

both father and monster in one noble effort. Alta is alive and so is the rescue crew, ready to leave Altair-4 forever and return to the quaint green grass of home.

Gary J. Svehla

Frankenstein
Universal 1931; Director: James Whale

Universal's adaptation of Mary Shelley's classic Gothic novel remains the definitive version, despite all the cinematic permutations of the book since then. Viewing *Frankenstein* today, it is hard to believe that the film was made over 75 years ago. Whale's celebrated and groundbreaking horror movie could easily have been a product of the 1950s or early 1960s, such was his brilliance behind the camera; long shots, close-ups, angled shots, swift cutting from one piece of action to another, unorthodox lighting. All the hallmarks of a master technician at work. And then there's the set design; Frankenstein's castle with its high, vaulted stone walls and dark, twisting stairways, the opulence on show at the scientist's wedding, the period village and the old mill. Karloff's monster has never been bettered, not even in Universal's follow-ups, the actor displaying an innate sense of mime, particularly in the scene where Colin Clive opens a shutter to allow the sunlight in, Karloff gazing up at the light like a child, hands held out in a beseeching gesture to his creator, as the shutter is closed. The only thing that's missing from the production is a suitable soundtrack to underline Whale's startling imagery, obviously influenced by early German cinema and the likes of *The Phantom of the Opera* (1925). Several scenes cut through censorship (the monster impaling his tormentor, hunchback Dwight Frye, on a hook; Clive shouting in exultation "It's alive! It's alive!" and references to Clive usurping God's power, as his creation lifts an arm; and Karloff throwing a little girl into the lake, when he runs out of flower heads) were restored in later prints. Jack Pierce's makeup job on Karloff is without doubt the most iconic monster design of all time. It takes 30 minutes of screen time before Frankenstein's creation makes its first appearance, Karloff's bulky frame fills the doorway to Clive's laboratory, as he lumbers in backward, and turns slowly. Whale executes a three-zoom shot on those limpid eyes and heavy scarred brow, the monster stiffly walks over to a chair in front of Frankenstein's guests, fiancée (Mae Clarke), friend John Boles and professor Edward Van Sloan to perform his party tricks. Escaping from the castle, the Creature (which possesses a damaged brain) gate-crashes Clive's wedding, murders the little girl by the lake and is tracke to a derelict mill, where it perishes in an inferno, after hurling Frankenstein to the ground. Bela Lugosi was originally earmarked to play the role of the Monster (the Hungarian actor initially thought he was going to play Dr. Frankenstein), but after seeing his awkward attempt at the role in *Frankenstein Meets the Wolf Man*, it's just as well that he didn't, although Lugosi himself wasn't keen on the part because it was silent. Almost akin to a very nightmarish fairy tale, *Frankenstein*'s overall look and texture has echoed down through the decades, one of horror's key works; despite moments of primitiveness, the movie belies its age. It has certainly worn better than Universal's other landmark horror film from this period, Tod Browning's *Dracula*.

Barry Atkinson

Frankenstein and the Monster from Hell
Paramount, 1974; Director: Terence Fisher

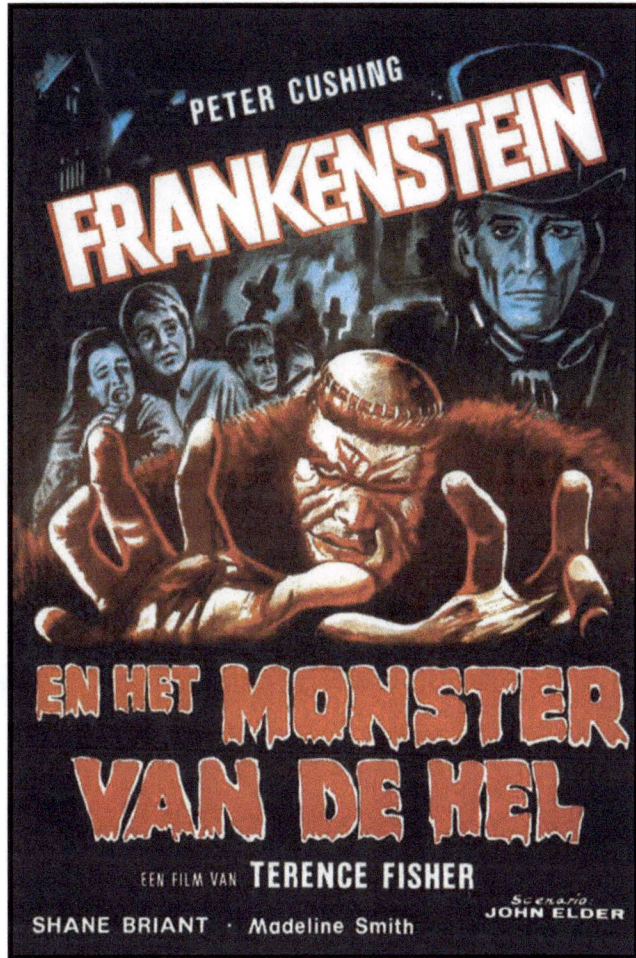

Hammer's seventh and final *Frankenstein* picture reunited Terence Fisher (who was brought out of semi-retirement), Peter Cushing and composer James Bernard in what would turn out to be a final attempt to return to the superlative values of the company's glory years and their Gothic roots (1955-1962), and in the main they succeeded. Set almost entirely within the bleak walls of an asylum for the criminally insane, Cushing plays Dr. Karl Victor, an alias for Baron Frankenstein, wielding unchallenged authority over both the inmates and the staff. Madeline Smith is his winsome, mute assistant, joined by young Shane Briant, incarcerated in the asylum on a charge of sorcery. The monster that Cushing is creating in his spare time, a Neanderthal-looking hulking brute (Dave Prowse), has the body of an insane killer, the hands of an artist and the brain of a violin-playing professor. Yes, it was a well-worn route that Fisher headed down, but *Frankenstein and the Monster from Hell*, although solemn in tone and directed with cold, clinical precision by Fisher, is a vastly underrated horror film, adding to, rather than diminishing, the *Frankenstein* myth. Twenty years on from his first starring role as the Baron, Cushing, dressed immaculately in black, portrayed the Baron with an icy malevolence, cold-eyed and cold-hearted, repeating his by now futile experiments in order to create the perfect being, his somber demeanor matching the careful color cinematography—stark grays for the asylum and greenish hues for the Baron's laboratory. The grisly brain surgery sequence is worthy of inclusion in any of the gore-slasher movies that were to follow, and although the creature looked a composite shambles, Prowse managed to bring out the pathos lurking within the beast—the monster picking up a violin and trying to play it before crushing the instrument, and his efforts in scribbling out mathematical equations on a blackboard before sending it flying and asking to be fed. Briant, being groomed by Hammer as a leading man before the company's unfortunate demise, made a personable assistant who turns against Cushing when he learns that the Baron plans to mate the monster with the mute Smith, who was raped as a small girl by her father, the alcoholic head of the asylum. The sudden gory climax sees the monster torn to shreds by the deranged inmates, and Cushing, with a shrug of his shoulders, informing his two assistants that he has already thought of ideas for his next creation. The film was not a great success. This was 1974, remember, and long-gone were the days when the public queued up in their droves to catch the latest British horror movie, besides *The Exorcist* was grabbing all the headlines, consigning Hammer's *Frankenstein* effort to the cinematic equivalent of the bargain-basement. Thirty years on, the movie can be appreciated for what it was—a superior, meaty slice of Hammer Horror, not perhaps up to the standards set by *The Curse of Frankenstein* or *The Revenge of Frankenstein*, but far worthier than what came after, or, in some cases, what had gone before, and that includes *The Horror of Frankenstein*, one of the company's all-time stinkers.

Barry Atkinson

Frankenstein's Daughter
Astor, 1958; Director: Richard E. Cunha

Richard Cunha's cheapo horror flick doesn't owe its allegiance to any other *Frankenstein* movie (except, perhaps, *I Was a Teenage Frankenstein*); instead, it's a glorious example of "schlock-horror" at its campy best, an insane mix of teenagers, Jekyll and Hyde, mad doctors and the 1950s ugliest Mary Shelley creation. Even before the credits roll, we're treated to the sight of a deranged women in a nightdress running at the

camera, with wild hair, thick bushy eyebrows, bulbous staring eyes and decaying, protruding teeth. Who, or what, is it? It's Sandra Knight, whose elderly uncle (Felix Locher) is a doctor experimenting with a drug that will halt the aging process. His jumped-up assistant, Oliver Frank (Donald Murphy), turns out to be a very distant descendant of Dr. Frankenstein, so while Murphy is helping the doctor with his experiments, he is also creating a monster in the underground laboratory *and* creating his own lethal cocktail of drugs, spiking Knight's drinks and turning her into a grotesque, shaggy-haired she-devil. Knight's one and only transformation scene is effectively handled by Cunha; collapsing onto her bed after unwittingly downing her drugged fruit punch, dark circles appear under her eyes, her skin creases, she begins to look very ill, the teeth grow and her eyes are like two tennis balls (apparently, according to publicity, the actress almost fainted when she saw herself in a mirror after veteran makeup man Harry Thomas had finished with her). Meanwhile, Murphy's creation in the basement has one vital piece missing—the head, not the bloody hand that his moronic gardener/assistant brings him. Lusting after blonde Sally Todd, Murphy takes her on a date; she spurns his lecherous advances and, in anger, he runs her down, stitching her mangled head onto his monster which then breaks out of the lab in a black PVC suit and goes on a mini-rampage, before returning to its creator. Soon after, Locher is taken into custody on a fabricated theft charge, leaving Murphy in charge of the house, and he wants Knight's brain in the monster's head! In the closing minutes, as the police arrive, John Ashley (Knight's boyfriend) throws a vial of acid into Murphy's face, as the madman tries to operate on the girl; the monster catches fire and goes up in flames. As usual with the lower-budget horror movies of the 1950s, Cunha had to include a rock 'n' roll interlude near the end to keep the kids (but not the adults) amused, but considering Astor knocked this out in a week at a cost of $60,000, *Frankenstein's Daughter* is an enjoyable 85-minutes of monster hokum, briskly directed by Cunha with enough ghoulish incidents to keep the interest going.

Barry Atkinson

Frankenstein Meets the Wolf Man
Universal, 1943; Director: Roy William Neill

The first of Universal's *Frankenstein* flicks to feature more than one monster (the so-called Monster Rally movies) is an all-out winner, one of the finest in the series with one notable drawback—Bela Lugosi's backhanded interpretation of the Frankenstein monster. Slick and fast-paced, the movie kicks off in grand 1940s fashion. Two grave-robbers in a windy cemetery break into the Talbot family crypt and pry open the lid from Lawrence Talbot's tomb, foolishly brushing aside the wolfbane from his still-fresh corpse (even though he's been buried four years), therefore reviving the cursed Lon Chaney, Jr. Waking up in a Cardiff hospital, the full moon brings on the first of Chaney, Jr.'s three transformations in the movie, and they're more effectively executed than in *The Wolf Man*, showing much greater detail in the laps and dissolves as Chaney goes on a rampage, kills a police officer and reawakens in the hospital, dazed and confused. Doctor Patric Knowles puts him in a straightjacket, thinking the man insane with his preposterous stories of

"changing into an animal," but Chaney, Jr. rips through his bonds, locates old Gypsy woman Maria Ouspenskaya (who understands his affliction) and off they go to Vasaria, in her wagon, in the hope that Baron Frankenstein can cure Chaney, or at least give him a permanent release from his curse. Changing into the Wolf Man again, Chaney attacks a local girl. The villagers (including Universal regulars Lionel Atwill and Dwight Frye) think it was the work of the Frankenstein Monster, which Chaney and Ouspenskaya have discovered in an icy cavern under Frankenstein's ruined castle. Knowles has also followed the pair from Wales (how in the blazes did Chaney, Jr. and the Gypsy woman get that cart across the English Channel?) and the three team up with the Baron's daughter (Ilona Massey); she knows the whereabouts of her dead father's diary and can offer help to Chaney, Jr. Lugosi, who turned down the part of the monster in 1931 as he didn't fancy a non-speaking part, played the mute creature here with his arms outstretched, strutting in a stiff gait, hissing and snarling. Audiences never realized that the monster was supposed to be blind, references to this were cut from the final print (as were scenes of Knowles restoring the Monster's sight). All in all, it remains Lugosi's worst-ever performance (he was dropped by Universal shortly after completion) and no attempt is made to disguise the fact that stuntman Eddie Parker was the monster in the more strenuous scenes, principally of the Wolf Man and the Monster fighting to the death. The climatic laboratory sequence has Knowles, against Massey's advice, deciding to ignore Chaney, Jr.'s plea for a merciful death and he pumps more electrical energy into Lugosi. Massey pulls a lever, the lab goes up in flames and a villager dynamites the dam; the two monsters, battling it out, are swept away on a tidal wave of mud and debris. Mention must be made of Hans J. Salter's score, his rousing title theme is the series' best (shared with *House of Frankenstein*, which he also scored). Salter's imaginative, melodious soundtracks are now largely forgotten highlights of many of the old Universal horror classics, genuine mini-symphonies in their own right, an art form that sadly has faded into obscurity from modern-day cinema features. *Frankenstein Meets the Wolf Man* revived the flagging series after the dull *Ghost of Frankenstein,* and yet more monsters were added to the follow-up, 1944's *House of Frankenstein.*

Barry Atkinson

Frankenstein 1970
Allied Artists, 1958; Director: Howard W. Koch

A terrified young woman runs through darkened woods, pursued by the lurching Frankenstein Monster, with clawed hands. Reaching a misty lake, she plunges in, closely followed by the monster, who grabs her and forces her under the water. Then a voice yells "Cut!" Yes, it's a film crew celebrating 230 years of the Frankenstein legend by making a movie, at Baron Frankenstein's castle no less. It's a pity, then, that the following 80 minutes of *Frankenstein 1970* didn't live up to the brilliant opening five minutes. What follows is a rather pedestrian reworking of the old tale, enlivened by the solid presence of horror legend Boris Karloff, playing a descendant of the original Frankenstein. Karloff was one of those rare actors who could always be relied on to turn in a pleasing performance, whatever he appeared in, and he virtually carries the whole of this picture on his own. Another plus is the CinemaScope photography, in crisp black and white, which was a real treat for fans in those days, often making the most routine of productions worth the price of a ticket, and this was no exception. Baron Karloff, scarred, limping and bitter from

around and giving the crew the jitters simply by looking at them. After bumping off his manservant to give his creation a new heart, two members of the crew are killed before the Monster receives a pair of eyes from Karloff's confidante. Until then, the six-foot plus Monster, swathed in bandages from head to foot and as blind as a bat, simply lumbers around the vaults, partly in shadow, becoming a nuisance. The climax sees Karloff and his Monster perishing in a cloud of radioactive steam from his atomic reactor. When police peel the bandages off the frazzled creature, the face resembles a younger Baron, who was trying to create the being in his own image. Paul Dunlap's full-blooded score was better than usual for this kind of run-of-the-mill fare, and there were one or two imaginative touches conjured up by director Koch (a photographer, panning the vaults through his lens, focuses unexpectedly on the huge bandaged form before him); moreover, the picture was popular enough to run for years in the U.K., more often than not paired with the same company's incredibly mundane thriller *Macabre*.

Barry Atkinson

The Ghost
Magna Pictures, 1963; Director: Robert Hampton/Riccardo Freda

The Ghost, directed by Riccardo Freda (billed as Robert Hampton for American distribution), illustrates both the strengths and the flaws inherent in the Euro-Gothic genre. Freda, Mario Bava's mentor, creates a widescreen Technicolor scarefest dripping in moody cinematography. Often times the camera almost becomes another character, as it explores the shadowy corridors of the spooky mansion, the underground burial vaults, etc. To me the balance is slightly askew as too much mood equals tedium, but connoisseurs of Euro horror seem to enjoy such diversions. Once again the plot is predictable, but story is always secondary to the cinematography and the intense psychologically driven characters. And by 1963, when this movie was made, Barbara Steele was a horror film icon (although in *The Ghost* she seems too thin with overdone eye makeup and a big hair wig that tends to draw attention away from her expressive mouth and eyes). The plot involves Dr. Hichcock (Leonard G. Elliott), his wife Margaret (Steele) and Hichcock's doctor Charles (Peter Baldwin). Hichcock suffers from a degenerative neurological disease, and as treatment, the physician Charles administers poison, with the antidote following quickly. However, Margaret and Charles are having an affair, so Hichcock is quickly killed off with the poison (minus the antidote). Soon a cat and mouse game involving the murdered man's riches and where they are hidden leads to suspicion and betrayal, especially when Hichcock's missing gems and jewelry are found falling out of Charles' medical bag. At the same time ghostly apparitions occurs swinging chandeliers, flying chess pieces and even the ghastly return of a decaying Hichcock, ultimately prompting Margaret's murder of her lover using a straight razor, as she slashes his

his experiences at the hands of the Nazis in the war, leases out his castle to the film crew, while creating a Creature in his atomic laboratory deep below the castle's crypts, hobbling face, arms and body, producing a wonderful shot where his blood drips down the camera lens as the viewer watches, in a subjective shot, the hateful intensity in the face of Margaret. Of course it turns out Hichcock is not dead, and using his faithful house servant as accomplice, Hichcock has concocted a plan for revenge by turning the smoldering passion between murderous lovers into mistrust and ultimately murder. But in the best tradition of treachery (based upon "The Pardoner's Tale" from *The Canterbury Tales*), in celebration, the good doctor drinks poison gin and dies a slow, tortuous death, as his wife also dies from poison, but she laughs hysterically as his perfect plan backfires and the police arrive. *The Ghost*, for me, disappoints as the plot is transparent, the mood and cinematography overdone and the characters little more than stereotypes. Better examples of this style of Euro horror exist, and in a movie running slightly over 90 minutes, more sequences of visitations from the dead are needed to generate horror.

Gary J. Svehla

Hand of Death
20th Century Fox, 1962; Director: Gene Nelson

One of the last theatrical science fiction/horror movies that Universal favorite John Agar ever appeared in, *Hand of Death* is a real curio of the genre. After all, how often is it that you get to see a 59-minute black-and-white horror film made in CinemaScope? Not often is the answer, as this remains a little-seen effort from Fox, only appearing in Britain in 1966 on a double bill with *The Cabinet of Caligari* on the Sunday one-day program circuit before disappearing without a trace. The plot itself is pretty flimsy, scarcely lending itself to a longer running time, just under one hour. Out in the desert, research scientist Agar and his assistant are working on an experimental nerve gas that, when rendered to armed forces in times of war, will, Agar hopes, knock them out before putting them into a hypnotic trance, obedient to those around them. After getting the go-ahead to carry on with his experimentation from the head of the Los Angeles Research Institution, he unfortunately falls asleep in his laboratory, while the room is filled with the vapor; on waking up, his skin itches but otherwise there appears to be no side effects—at first. Then he has an argument with his assistant, grabs the man and kills him with his corrosive touch. Setting fire to the lab, Agar flees to his boss' house, where he demands an antidote be produced for the symptoms of the gas. However, Agar then transforms into something resembling a grotesque, bloated pumpkin, the startling after-effects of breathing in the gas. Killing the doctor with his burning, puffy fingers, Agar dons trenchcoat and fedora hat and goes on the run, deranged by his condition. After his distressed girlfriend has pleaded with him to give himself up, the police corner him on a beach and shoot him to death. There is very little cinematic finesse in evidence when Agar becomes pumpkin man, simply scenes show him lurching along roads and staggering across the beach in his disguise, and if this was one of the company's lower-budgeted horror flicks, then they really didn't do John Agar or the plotline justice. But the actor, even in the brief time he is on screen, before becoming the deformed killer, is as personable as ever and virtually carries the picture on his own.

Barry Atkinson

The Haunted Strangler
British Amalgamated/MGM, 1958; Director: Robert Day

Boris Karloff starred in all manner of horror movies after leaving Universal International, and this ranks as one of the more interesting. Also known as *Grip of the Strangler*, the film can be viewed as a murder mystery, a horror thriller, a take on the Jack the Ripper legend or a Jekyll and Hyde-type drama—or all four! The film opens with the graphic hanging of the so-called Haymarket Strangler, outside the forbidding walls of Newgate Prison in 1880. The callous crowd of onlookers enjoy the spectacle as the movie jumps forward 20 years. Karloff is a novelist obsessed with the idea that the wrong man, a Dr. Styles, was hanged for these killings; he reckons it should have been a Dr. Tennant charged with the murders, who was present at the autopsy before disappearing, leaving his surgeon's knife in the coffin. The police, the prison governor, Karloff's wife and daughter and his assistant think that he's mad to carry out this needless research into a long-dead crime, but Karloff persists, determined to get to the bottom of the mystery. Bribing a prison guard to open Styles' coffin, he finds the surgical instrument hidden among the bones and suddenly, knife in hand, he changes into a psychopathic killer himself. The transformation scenes are eerily effective, requiring little in the way of dissolves or makeup. Tennant suffered from paralysis down his left side, as Karloff does now, his face screwing up, his left arm twisting awkwardly and his body hunched, lank hair drooping over his maniacal features. Half strangling and stabbing a showgirl to death in a nearby theater, Karloff reverts back to his normal self but slowly begins to realize that *he* may be the doctor, this being the deep-rooted reason for his obsessive behavior. His long-suffering wife (Jean Kent) confirms that 20 years ago, she encountered the young Tennant in a hospital, took pity on his condition and ended up marrying him; [SPOILER ALERT] Karloff is, in fact, Tennant! Strangling his wife to death for her revelations, Karloff is arrested and locked up in an asylum, but he breaks free from his straitjacket, confessing all to his daughter and assistant before the police chase him to Style's grave. Shot down, he places the knife in the earth, covering the grave and dies. Photographed in grainy monochrome to enhance the grimy Victorian backdrops and paying realistic attention to time and place, *The Haunted Strangler* over-emphasizes the brutality meted out in the prison whipping scenes. Day's grim little chiller was made in tandem with the inferior *Corridors of Blood* (also starring Karloff) and remains one of the director's most striking pieces of work from this lean period in British horror filmmaking. Karloff is simply superb in the title role.

Barry Atkinson

Horrors of the Black Museum
American International, 1959; Director: Arthur Crabtree

One of my fondest childhood movie experiences was seeing the ultra-violent *Horrors of the Black Museum* in a theater, when I was nine years old. However, in recent years, seeing the movie in faded and battered 16mm panned-and-scanned versions, the movie never holds up to that initial, favorable memory. But now restored to DVD with intense color, that initial cinematic experience can be replicated.

Horrors of the Black Museum was probably producer/co-screenwriter Herman Cohen's biggest financial success for American International, and it created the artistic green light for the studio to give Roger Corman a larger budget and the go-ahead to produce his Vincent Price/Poe series in widescreen and color. The true strength of *Horrors of the Black Museum* is the introduction of Michael Gough as a new horror film villain, a performance to be repeated in Cohen's *Konga, The Black Zoo* and *Trog*. Gough, who a year before played the doting brother, the reluctant hero, in Hammer's *Horror of Dracula*, is now recast with tri-color hair, a creepy

limp with short cane (and personality to match) and the ability to deliver dramatically even the most trivial, inane dialogue. Gough chews up the scenery, but does so in such a way that his performance makes him a truly memorable mad scientist villain. And he's never been more maniacal than his stellar performance in *Horrors of the Black Museum*. Following the basic story hook Cohen introduced in his teenage epics, such as *I Was a Teenage Frankenstein* and *I Was a Teenage Werewolf*, we have an older, wizened madman who takes a young impressionable male under his wing, and after building up the sense of trust, abuses that trust and uses drugs to turn the young, innocent male into a monster, one who does the elder's bidding.

Making full use of its gaudy EastmanColor photography, *Horrors of the Black Museum* features a slew of grisly murders, mostly executed on beautiful, sexy young women—a woman has her eyeballs pierced by spiked binoculars, another blonde beauty is beheaded by a portable guillotine propped above her bed and an elderly woman (who runs a curio shop) gets her throat punctured by huge ice tongs (with Gough grimacing all the way), etc. Other horrific sequences obviously thrown in for good measure include a horrific ride through the tunnel of love at an amusement part, a disfigured maniac with a knife jumps off the giant Ferris wheel and a murder victim is dipped into the vat of acid and reduced to bone. It's all sordid and overbaked, perfect for the youth horror market back in 1959. And while such mayhem might become dull and repetitive, Michael Gough's acting never allows that. Using the frame of Gough's Bancroft character, playing a newspaper writer whose column focuses on grisly crime, Gough becomes an annoying man who haunts the offices of Scotland Yard to get gory details of the latest violent crime or murder. But unknown to Scotland Yard, Bancroft is a collector of esoteric weapons and presides over his hidden Black Museum, where he displays his tribute to mayhem. Gough uses mad science to turn an innocent teenager into a violent fiend, one who does his bidding, especially murder.

As black and white teenaged-dominated drive-in theater horror of the 1950s was becoming colorized, more violent and geared toward adult audiences, *Horrors of the Black Museum* becomes the perfect bridge horror movie, melding the simplistic horrors of one decade to the more complex terrors of the next.

Gary J. Svehla

Glenn Strange as the Monster; Boris Karloff as Dr. Neimann; Lon Chaney, Jr. as Larry Talbot

House of Frankenstein
Universal, 1944; Director: Erle C. Kenton

Following the success of *Frankenstein Meets the Wolf Man*, Universal decided to throw all their eggs into one basket by coming up with a horror mix that included Dracula, the Wolf Man, the Frankenstein Monster and a hunchback, not to mention Boris Karloff as crazed Dr. Neimann. "All Together! The Screen's Titans of Terror!" proclaimed the posters. Karloff and hunchback J. Carrol Naish escape from Neustadt Prison during a storm, waylay George Zucco's traveling "House of Horrors" and murder Zucco, Karloff taking on his identity to elude the authorities. One of the exhibits is the skeleton of Dracula, displayed in his coffin. Karloff decides to remove the stake, thus reviving the vampire, on condition Dracula does as he bids. The first 20 minutes or so of the picture suffers a bit here. A cadaverous-looking John Carradine, in top hat and tails, is not a very scary bloodsucker, even though effects ace John P. Fulton has him changing into a bat. After he is trapped in the sun's rays and reverts back to a skeleton the pace picks up with the arrival of Lon Chaney, Jr., as the cursed Lawrence Talbot (the Wolf Man), and the Frankenstein Monster (played by Glenn Strange), both discovered by Karloff in an icy cavern underneath Frankenstein's ruined castle. Introduced into the plot is a tragic love triangle of sorts. A young Gypsy girl (Elena Verdugo) falls for the dejected-looking Chaney, Jr., while deformed Naish worships the ground she walks on. It all ends unhappily, of course. Karloff, intent on reactivating the Frankenstein Monster in his own laboratory, casually dismisses Chaney's pleas to help him get rid of the curse of lycanthropy, and he also ignores Naish's similar requests to operate on his deformed back. When the full moon rises, Chaney undergoes transformation into the Wolf Man and pounces on the Gypsy girl, just as she shoots him with a silver bullet; both end up dead. Grief-stricken after seeing the girl's body, Naish half-strangles Karloff in retribution for her loss and is then thrown out of a window, to his death, by a revived Glenn Strange. As the villagers storm Karloff's castle, the Frankenstein Monster drags Karloff off to the woods, where they both sink in a quagmire. This fine, old-fashioned monster yarn was boosted by Hans J. Salter's almost classical, rousing score and was such a big box-office hit that practically the whole crew and cast were back within the same year for *House of Dracula*.

Barry Atkinson

House of Wax
Warner Bros., 1953; Director: Andre de Toth

Imagine the scenario over 50 years ago: a darkened auditorium in England, 1954. The trailer to the X-rated *House of Wax* appears, all one minute of it (a strict censorial code in those days). A gloomy, fog-shrouded street. David Buttolph's spine-tingling music. The camera pans up to an open window and enters the bedroom. Phyllis Kirk lies in bed, asleep. A shadow of a man wearing a hat and cape appears slowly on her wall. She wakes up and screams. End of trailer. That brief snippet, together with reports of faintings in cinemas throughout the country, leads to a hideously scarred madman unmasked in the final reel, in 3-D to boot! Couple this with most people's innate dread of the morbid aura surrounding

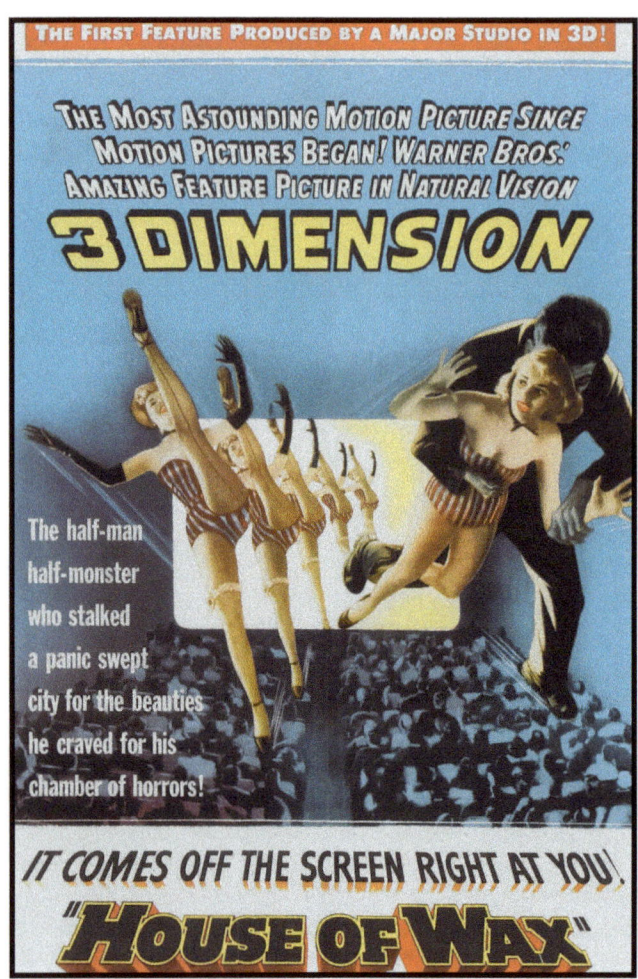

wax effigies (in particular Madame Tussaud's *Chamber of Horrors* in London)—all this contributed to Warner Bros. remake of *Mystery of the Wax Museum*. *House of Wax* became a massive box-office hit and as good an example of full-blooded 1950s Gothic-horror as you'll ever get. Vincent Price, previously in a series of dramatic costume dramas such as *The Private Lives of Elizabeth and Essex* (1939) and *Dragonwyck* (1946), was commanding in the role of sculptor Henry Jarrod, a gifted artist that is the victim of an insurance scam; his partner sets fire to the sculptor's lovingly rendered figures of historical men and women, leaving Price insane, disfigured and bent on revenge. To bring in the revenue, Price is forced to create a House of Wax that exhibits scenes of famous murders and murderers, including new crimes straight from the headlines to shock the public. Wheelchair-bound Price becomes fixated with Kirk, picturing her as his beloved Marie Antoinette. He stalks the woman, most notably in the famous sequence where the supposedly crippled sculptor hobbles after Kirk through the misty gas-lit city streets, like an avenging angel of death. Another eerie scene occurs is in the morgue following the strangulation of squeaky voiced Carolyn Jones. Two attendants leave the darkened room with its rows of sheet-covered corpses. Then Price sits up suddenly, his sheet slipping to reveal his grotesque features in half-light. As usual, the police are shown to be utterly incompetent (Frank Lovejoy and Dabbs Greer are the two hapless officers), and Kirk's boyfriend, a promising young sculptor (Paul Picerni), is just as clueless, refusing to give credence to Kirk's belief that human corpses lie underneath Price's wax figures. The unmasking climax in garish WarnerColor is a nightmarish classic, Price's domineering height and mellifluous tones contrasting chillingly with his ravaged face. Although, his melted features have been seen throughout the first part of the movie, this doesn't lessen the impact. Buttolph's oft-overlooked music (he provided the soundtrack to *The Beast from 20,000 Fathoms*) is almost a blueprint of how a Gothic horror film *should* be scored, with a brilliant opening title theme that counts as one of the decade's finest. The picture was reissued in England in 1978, screened in London in its original 3-D format and, although nobody passed out in their seats *this* time round. It was a treat to have those hideous features leap out and stare right at you—although the gimmicky ping-pong ball man sould have been left on the cutting room floor. A seminal horror picture indeed, as important to the genre as Hammer's early output and the movie that put Price on the road to horror from then on.

Barry Atkinson

The Invisible Man
Universal, 1933; Director: James Whale
The Invisible Man Returns
Universal, 1940; Director: Joe May
The Invisible Man's Revenge
Universal, 1944; Director: Ford Beebe
The Invisible Woman
Universal, 1940; Director: A. Edward Sutherland
The Invisible Agent
Universal, 1942; Director: Edwin L. Marin

Let the truth be known! James Whale and Terence Fisher are my two favorite horror film directors and I love

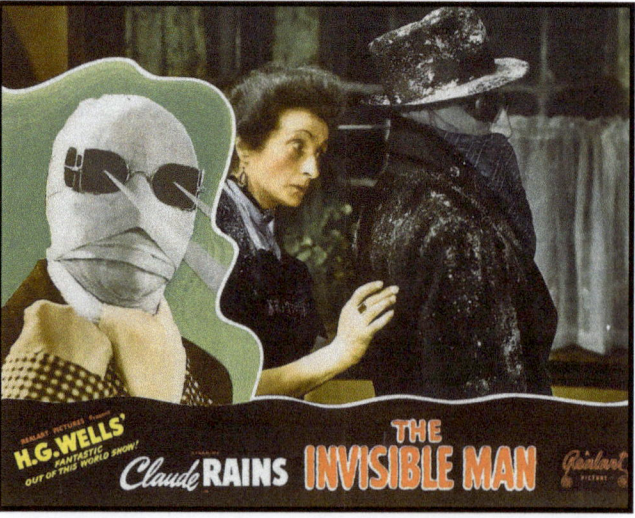

Una O'Connor welcomes the strange lodger (Claude Rains).

Frankenstein, *Bride of Frankenstein*, and *The Old Dark House*. However, *The Invisible Man*, for me, is the Universal clunker and the absolute worst of 1930s horror. There, I said it.

James Whale's *The Invisible Man* still warrants three stars and is a good film, but it is also a distressingly frustrating and ultimately disappointing classic. For once I find the contradiction in tone between the snowy entrance of Jack Griffin wrapped in gauze booking a room at the inn—the sequence played for true mystery and horror—and latter sequences of an over-the-top maniac dancing in his shirt tops and chasing goofy Keystone cops around the room jarring. The blending of horror and humor works to maximum satisfaction in *Bride of Frankenstein* and *The Old Dark House*, but in *The Invisible Man* it seems both grating and silly.

First, what works in the movie is the photography, performances by the leads (Claude Rains, Una O'Connor, Gloria Stuart and William Harrigan) and Whale's direction in those sequences that create a dank and ominous mood. I admit my bias favors horror over science fiction, and while John P. Fulton's special effects are exceptional for the time, another flaw of the movie is Whale's focusing too heavily on the silly effects that appear very dated today. The best special effect in the movie is Claude Rains' heavily made-up visage, his white bandaged face and chin, his darkened glasses and his gloved hands, all shot in intense close-up, making Jack Griffin's presence impossible to ignore. And Rains' line readings, his dialogue bellowing from a small body, create a performance based upon voice and bandages, and it is a dynamite iconic performance that spices up at best a good vehicle. The sequences at the inn with Griffin demanding to be left alone to finish his work, with the Cockney-voiced supporting players responding with suspicion and fear, peaks the dramatic tension in the first quarter of the movie. Not until Griffin invades the home of Dr. Kemp (William Harrigan) and literally forces the sniveling scientist to become his brother in arms (to conquer the world and lead its dominions) does the drama return to that intensity again. In one gripping sequence Kemp calls the police, but a car carrying love interest Flora (Gloria Stuart) and Dr. Cranley (Henry Travers) first pulls up in plain sight of Griffin. Griffin immediately accuses Kemp of calling the police and betraying him, creating suspense that builds until Griffin escapes through the hands-held police cordon. Threatening to kill Kemp at 10 o'clock thefollowing evening, Griffin finds the disguised Kemp alone in his getaway car and sends his former colleague and vehicle off a cliff (Griffin at first detailing all the pain and bodily damage Kemp will sustain before his neck is broken), the car explodes midway down the embankment.

Surprisingly, the film's pacing is lethargic and the plot spends too much time on upset citizenry and snoopy police stalking the wilderness for their invisible man. The film's tone is goofy, quaint and comical when the film needs to be suspenseful, spooky and dark. While James Whale's direction in key scenes is spot on, in many others, he seems to miss his

Invisible man Jon Hall confronts scientist John Carradine.

mark and allows tedium and mediocrity to rule. Fortunately supporting players E.E. Clive and Una O'Connor, presented for their comic shenanigans, are wonderfully drawn because their humorous antics are always laced with dread, fear and horror, not comedy for its own sake.

For instance, Universal's direct sequel, *The Invisible Man Returns*, is most remembered for its wonderfully green, and classic, one-sheet poster rather than for the production itself. Even with a cast comprised of Cedric Hardwicke, Nan Gray, Vincent Price and Cecil Kellaway, under Joe May's direction, *The Invisible Man Returns* is predictable. Geoffrey (Vincent Price), accused of murdering his brother, awaits execution while seedy and shifty-eyed cousin Cobb (Cedric Hardwicke) makes a phone call and sadly announces he cannot do anything to stay the execution, even though he has friends in high places. Cobb's guilt is established early in the film, and when Frank Griffin, brother to the original movie's Jack Griffin, goes to visit the death row prisoner hours before his execution, and Geoffrey disappears with only a pile of his clothes left behind in the jail cell, audiences know exactly what has happened. Geoffrey, now invisible, must solve his brother's murder to clear himself before the invisibility drug, now called duocane, makes him insane as it did his brother Jack. Even amid the interesting mining locale with high hill tracks, the suspense is minimal, performances are adequate and the direction lethargic. The gimmick of invisibility created by John Fulton may have fascinated at the time, but today, the shirt and trousers dancing playfully about or a suspended newspaper floating in air is not a special effect for all time (however Cecil Kellaway's smoking a cigar, blowing smoke, and seeing the outline of Geoffrey and lurching for him *is*; another excellent sequence shows the invisible man barely visible in the rain). This B production does impress in several sequences, though. One of the film's best scenes occurs when police spray a house with smoky gas to make the invisible man visible, yet cleverly, Geoffrey disguises himself as a policeman, wearing a gas mask, so he seems like another cop in a household filled with policeman. Geoffrey approaches Helen (Nan Grey) and has her pretend to faint, so he can *rescue* her and take her outside to escape. Nice chills are generated here.

The film's best sequence is the eerie death of former night watchman Spears (Alan Napier), now superintendent (under Cobb, who will inherit the business from his brother Geoffrey and ignores all the safety precautions his brother initiated). After Geoffrey toys with Spears' car, he announces his presence, causing Spears to flee for his life into the woods, Geoffrey playfully laughing, pretending to be a ghost. Spears tells the truth, that Cobb was responsible for brother Michael's death. Geoffrey leaves Spears tied up in his mining home while he visits Cobb. In a stark sequence, Price holds a gun on Cobb, who is under protective custody, and forces him to leave the house. However, the fear Hardwicke generates makes this a powerhouse sequence. Geoffrey takes Cobb to the house where Spears is standing on a chair, a noose deliberately tied around his neck, and Spears confesses that Cobb killed Michael. But foolishly, Geoffrey never realized how easy it would be for Cobb to kick the chair out from under Spears, thus hanging and killing instantly the only witness to the crime.

Overall, the film meanders without much horror or suspense, but in these few sequences the power of Vincent

Price's vocal performance dominates. (The sequence with Helen, Frank and Geoffrey having supper, Geoffrey dapper in dressing robe and bandages, becomes a high point, with Geoffrey revealing his disdain for feeble humanity and the hopes he has of becoming an all powerful ruler. Such a sequence is a tribute to Vincent Price, the actor.) *The Invisible Man Returns* is not even a great B production, but it does feature sequences of dramatic intensity that make it quite enjoyable.

The third sequel, *The Invisible Man's Revenge,* directed by Ford Beebe in 1944, features Jon Hall in his first starring role in Universal's invisibility entry. Taking a decidedly film noir nod, Hall, who escapes from a dockside ship, buys new clothing from an elderly haberdasher who asks too many questions, forcing the mysterious man, Robert Griffin, to get defensive and overbearing. Soon grabbing hold of his emotions, he politely exits but leaves behind a folded newspaper article showing him to be an escaped homicidal murderer with a blood trail in his recent past. Griffin returns to visit prim and proper Sir Jasper (Lester Matthews) and Lady Irene (Gale Sondergaard), Griffin having been left for dead in the jungle at the hands of the couple. The now wealthy duo benefited from finding a diamond mine there, but the agreement was that all three parties should share equally, and Griffin wants his cut. The other two claim the fortune is gone, wasted on bad investments. Griffin is not satisfied when Jasper offers to give him half of his personal cash resources. Soon they drug him and have him thrown off the property, but they keep his copy of the financial arrangement and want him out of the way, forever.

Griffin becomes a fugitive and seeks shelter at the home of Dr. Drury (John Carradine), whose eyes light up: "fugitive… no friends!" Griffin realizes things are strange when he sees an invisible dog in a cage and a birdcage swing with an invisible parrot squawking away. Soon loud barking occurs from outside and an invisible dog on a leash enters. Griffin volunteers to become the doctor's guinea pig and be turned invisible, but after the experiment proves successful, Griffin pushes the old doctor aside and heads toward Jasper's house to claim his fortune. Forcing Jasper to sign a confession, Griffin is almost clunked over the head but manages to elude a flying chair.

Griffin falls in love with the beautiful Julie (Evelyn Ankers, in a bland role) and wants to get pretty boy Mark (Alan Curtis) out of her life, even if that means murder. Discovering a full body blood transfusion will turn him temporarily visible, Griffin drains the doctor of all his blood and sets his home afire, seeking refuge at Sir Jasper's. He is joined by Cockney comic relief Herbert Higgins (Leon Errol), who wants a cut of the good life—but Griffin offers him money to kill the loyal hound of the dead doctor, who tracked the evil Griffin as far as Jasper's home, and waits outside howling and moaning.

The film's best moments occur near the end when Griffin, speaking to Julie and Mark, begins to turn invisible without warning. Cross-cutting shots of a transparent Jon Hall with

Classic screen actor, John Barrymore (left), nearing the end of his career, brings a zany performance to the film.

actor Jon Hall wearing heavy pancake makeup, the panicky victim runs to his room covering his head with a sweater and seeks refuge in the bathroom, his entire head now invisible. This leads to Griffin's scheme to lure Mark down to the wine cellar. To turn visible once again, Griffin plans to kill Mark by draining his body of blood. Julie will now be his once Mark is out of the way and Griffin is again visible. The thrilling climax features the locked-in Mark reacting to the invisible one's taunts, throwing of objects and finally finding himself overwhelmed and knocked unconscious with a bottle of wine. The invisible man almost manages to kill Mark, as Griffin turns semi-visible, but the police break through the cellar door and the persistent vicious dog attacks and kills Griffin. Once again, *The Invisible Man's Revenge* is perhaps a hair better than *The Invisible Man Returns*, even though the characters in *Revenge* are far less sympathetic. Both sequels are fine B productions, each offering 80-odd minutes of fun and excitement.

Surprisingly, Jon Hall played an undercover wartime spy two years earlier in 1942's *The Invisible Agent*, which is a pleasant surprise in the Invisible Man series. The movie, caught up in WWII Nazi spy shenanigans, features Hall as the grandson of the original Invisible Man, who keeps the formula hidden in his small print shop which is visited by five Nazi spies, including Stauffer (Cedric Hardwicke) and the Baron (Peter Lorre). Forcing Griffin to close his shop, the criminals want Griffin's invisibility formula to help their war effort, and they want it now. The Peter Lorre character notices a wonderful cutting blade on one piece of press equipment and forces Hall's hand underneath, he slowly presses down on the blade, forcing the poor victim to talk. Giving in to pressure, Griffin screams to stop the torture, shouting he will get them the formula, which he produces from a hidden department in his desk drawer. However, in the ruckus the front store window is smashed, and Griffin is able, with a few

Kathleen Burke (as The Panther Woman), Richard Arlen and Charles Laughton as Dr. Moreau

well-placed punches and kicks, to escape with the formula. He makes a deal with agents of the U.S. government—who want him to use the formula to turn one of their best agents invisible, Griffin insists he be made the guinea pig and carry out the mission.

In a wonderful special effects sequence, Griffin parachutes from the heavily bombarded plane, and as he slowly descends, he turns invisible with his harness and chute still descending. Griffin finally lands on a rooftop, where he escapes. Soon he is romancing the elegant Nazi character portrayed by Ilona Massey, who is ultimately revealed to be an American agent. During the course of events, Griffin again meets up with Cedric Hardwicke and Peter Lorre, who make effective villains. By the film's end Lorre commits hara-kiri with a knife and Griffin is rescued and returned to America, now with love interest Massey. But beforehand, the film features several marvelous special effects sequences, most impressively a sequence where Griffin dons a bathrobe and applies cream to his face and hands to be visible to Massey. Only the circles around his eyes remain invisible, but he dons dark glasses to finish the illusion. Unlike Jon Hall's character in *Revenge*, here in *The Invisible Agent* he is truly the pulp hero who is willing to sacrifice his life for the cause of freedom and the victory of the United States. It is a propaganda-filled B production, but it is one that approximates the thrills and chills of the world of serials, and this movie could have inspired an entire invisibility espionage series all by itself.

Finally, the most comical entry here, 1940's *The Invisible Woman*, features a fading John Barrymore and Virginia Bruce as the title character. Perhaps this is the least successful movie in the series (interestingly enough, the screenplay was written by the team most responsible for writing some of the best Abbott and Costello movie scripts) and is played for comedy effect only. Even though the reliable John P. Fulton is once again employed for the invisibility effects, generally here his bag of special effects tricks underwhelm. Perky Virginia Bruce is just right as Kitty, but even her required nude sequence behind the screen fails to sizzle. John Barrymore, reduced to ham-fisted roles in less spectacular movie projects, is really quite good in this underplayed heavily made-up performance. He plays the wacky scientist whose projects are undermined by the son of a wealthy patron, who has just gone broke from financial excess. Instead of being able to offer a volunteer $3,000 to be turned invisible, Professor Gibbs (Barrymore) can only offer the thrill, but no financial compensation. However that's enough for Kitty, who wants to use her momentary invisibility to gain revenge on the nasty boss who fired her from her modeling job, for speaking her mind.

The movie's minimal plot develops when a group of gangsters move in on the professor. This gang includes comic "Stooge" Shemp Howard, whose funniest scene involves him being knocked unconscious and wearing a fish bowl over his head. Also the gifted comedian Charles Ruggles plays the flippant and wisecracking butler George, but the role as written does not allow Ruggles much of an opportunity to dazzle.

The movie, light on comedy, special effects and plot, ends with a newborn baby suddenly turning invisible. Perhaps the best performance in the movie belongs to the fading John Barrymore, whose professor is warm, zany and comical, when needed to be. However, when compared to the other films in the series, this A. Edward Sutherland–directed B production is bare bones at best. Not even a too-small supporting role by Margaret Hamilton can save this non-entity.

Even though James Whale's *The Invisible Man* is a flawed Universal horror classic, featuring the least of all iconic monsters, the B series that followed is well worth the effort and manages to entertain and thrill.

Gary J. Svehla

Island of Lost Souls
Paramount, 1932; Director: Erle C. Kenton

Paramount pulled off the triple threat by merging elements of horror, science fiction and jungle thrillers in 1933's *Island of Lost Souls*. While not as celebrated as some of his fellow filmmakers, director Erle C. Kenton did a credible job maintaining suspense amid a menacing jungle backdrop. He does, however, struggle with some of the finer points of cinematic technique, including the use of sound.

Island of Lost Souls fumbles many opportunities to use sound creatively, a fact that is especially surprising for a film of this late vintage. An absence of background music dates the film and contributes to a ragged sense of pacing. Dialogue is a hit and miss affair; Charles Laughton's voicing of vainglorious Dr. Moreau is menacing and authoritative one minute, but flip and inappropriately giddy the next. As the film's nominal hero, Richard Arlen looks and sounds ill at ease, and Bela Lugosi, the Sayer of the Law, speaks in modulated tones that are hard to decipher. Helping to offset this are a couple of nice audio touches, including the ghastly cries of the manimals in Moreau's House of Pain and their half-human cries of vengeance during the film's gripping conclusion.

Visually, however, the film is a standout. Principal characters are often glimpsed in half shadow, illuminated by an unseen light source. An abundance of white interiors bathe scenes in a shimmering glow, reminiscent of the best of silent cinematography. Eye-catching also are the visual patterns of cages and bars seen throughout the film, images created by jungle foliage, window blinds or crisscrossing wood panels. Touches like these would have been doubly effective in a silent version, where such motifs were frequently used to compliment the action onscreen.

Given its visual orientation, the story offered interesting possibilities for a silent treatment. The film's action scenes and the unsettling ambiance of Moreau's hellish jungle would have translated well, especially if accentuated through the use of tinted film stock. Tinting was a technique commonly used by both major and minor studios to give a film an impressive, arty look. Colors were chosen to reflect time and setting— blue for night scenes, amber for daylight and red for fire. Although its usage began to taper off in the late 1920s, the practice continued until the widespread adaptation of the Fox sound-on-film system, which registered an audible pop in the presence of tinted film. (Various two-strip colors processes were also used during the late silent/early talkie period, but the practice remained a novelty until the development of three-strip Technicolor in the mid 1930s.) Had the exotic locale and shadowy horrors of H.G. Wells' tale been given this treatment, its nightmare world might have been rendered all the more vivid.

The visual touches seen in *Island of Lost Souls* are indeed effective, even if some of the directorial choices are not entirely original. (One camera shot, that of an enormous growing shadow, was lifted directly from Mamoulian's *Dr. Jekyll and Hyde*, but we must remember that noted cinematographer Karl Struss photographed both films.) Kenton and cinematographer Karl Struss use the jungle milieu to good advantage, creating some of the most disturbing visual tableaus of the early sound era. A silent version would have also benefited from their approach, especially when one takes into account the full range of visual tools available to filmmakers during that period. In this case, the absence of sound might not have been a significant liability.

Steven Thornton

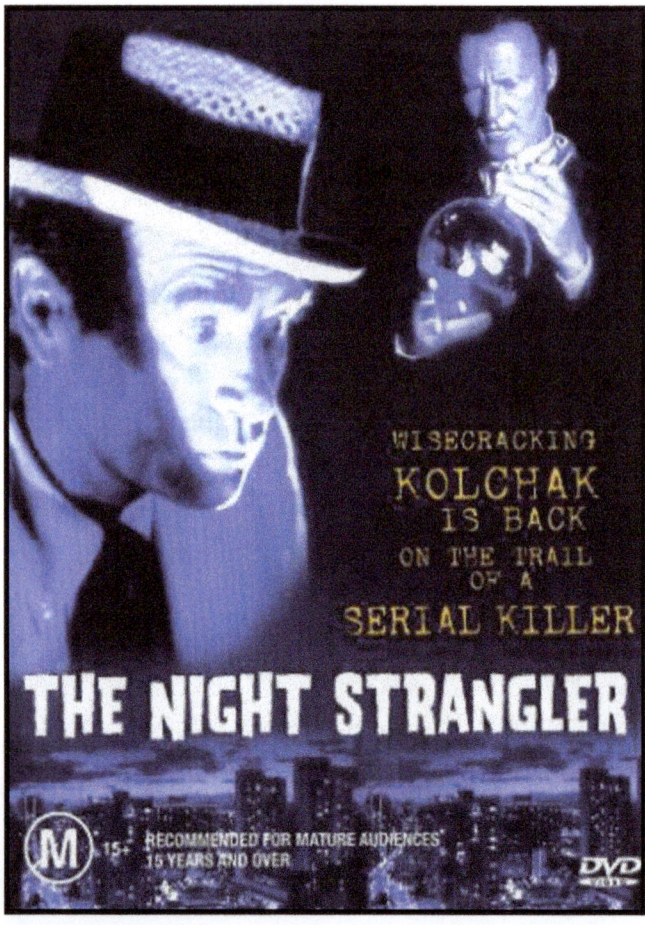

The Invisible Ray
Universal, 1936; Director: Lambert Hillyer

Perhaps the unsung gem of the classic horror Universal canon, *The Invisible Ray*, happens to be one of my favorite Universal horror movies (although its genesis is more by way of science fiction) and features equal performances (both stellar) by Boris Karloff and Bela Lugosi. For one thing, *The Invisible Ray* has a sense of scope. We start at Janos Rukh's home observatory, then move to the African jungle and finally end up in the city of Paris, with Rukh running amok. The character of Rukh is classic Karloff, at first showing the scientist to be the dedicated man of science, but soon his nobility fades as he is revealed to be an anti-social recluse who feels paranoid about his scientific discovery, quickly reverting, via the help of Radium X poisoning, into an avenging madman who kills methodically those people he holds responsible for stealing his discovery. Via John Fulton's inspired glowing special effects, Karloff radiates in the darkness and his simple touch spells instant death, unless he takes the antidote given him by his doubting Thomas rival Dr. Benet (Bela Lugosi). Karloff is sympathetic and deranged, while Lugosi, looking majestic in slicked-back hair and goatee, underplays his performance but still generates conflicting flashes of both ruthless detachment and compassion. The teaming of these horror icons is both inspired and totally satisfying, with neither actor upstaging the other and both performances becoming important ones.

The best sequences in the movie involve the teaming of Karloff and Violet Kemble Cooper as Mother Rukh, the stern white-haired woman who tells her son he is not good at dealing with people and should work alone in his laboratory. She is absolutely correct, but her lack of motherly sympathy and her hard-nosed life lessons make her a truly fascinating character. At the movie's end when Janos confronts her, pleading for comfort and advice, she flings her cane and smashes the bottle of antidote, spelling her son's destruction. He turns momentarily into a human fireball and burns away. Even among the veterans, Cooper contributes a performance equal to Karloff and Lugosi (albeit of much shorter duration).

For years people have criticized the direction of Lambert Hillyer, who is best known for directing B productions and serials. For me the charm of *The Invisible Ray* is its outrageous sense of sci-fi adventure theatrics. The movie contains complex characters with delicate problems. For instance, Rukh's wife Diana (Frances Drake) is much younger than he and admits she only married Rukh because her father, Rukh's now dead assistant, admired the scientist and wanted her to marry him (Freud would do wonders with these relationships). But Hillyer keeps the action pumping and the plot marching onward. Besides the jungle footage, discovering and harnessing Radium X, we also have the sidebar story of Rukh's wife falling for the young hunk in the pith helmet (Ronald Drake), thus explaining Rukh's impending insanity: He loses both his scientific formula and wife in one hot and muggy expedition (where all the actors are constantly sweating). But once Rukh disappears and is presumed dead, the real fun begins as the demented avenging angel kills each member of the expedition, one at a time. For once a film's pacing and performances go hand in hand to produce an outstanding Universal horror epic that is long overdue recognition as the wonderful chiller it most certainly is. And as stated, Karloff and Lugosi have never been better balanced. Also, it is indeed refreshing to see Boris Karloff create a broad, over-the-top performance, much in the standard Lugosi style, and do it as well as Lugosi.

Gary J. Svehla

Kolchak: The Night Strangler
ABC, 1973; Director: Dan Curtis

While I originally preferred *The Night Strangler* (the sequel, again returning Kolchak to investigate a series of strangulations near Underground Seattle) to the original *Night Stalker*, upon subsequent viewings, I have to give the nod to the original. However, the 1973 sequel is almost as good, and at 90 minutes it still sustains interest throughout.

For the sequel Darren McGavin sports better-styled (and lighter) hair, but he still wears his seersucker suit and plays the role of arrogant coward to the hilt. Again working with his gruff newspaper editor Simon Oakland, the rapport between the formerly bitter adversaries is more close-knit in the sequel, as both are under the power of newspaper magnate John Carradine, who ultimately has both men fired and on the road by the final scene.

The Night Strangler follows the formula of its predecessor much too closely, for we have beautiful young women murdered and their blood drained by a hundred-year-old doctor, who in the best tradition of *The Man in Half Moon Street/The Man Who Could Cheat Death*, uses a blood serum to maintain immortality. His formula is flawed and he needs a new infusion of blood and formula every 21 years. Richard Anderson plays the fiend, but he only has one sequence near the end of the movie where he gets to perform and establish his character. In every other sequence he is merely depicted as a shadowy figure that preys on innocent victims on the foggy streets of Seattle. And quite stupidly, before he takes his potion, he allows Kolchak time to throw a projectile at the bubbling vial and break it, thus destroying the formula. *The Night Strangler* did not inspire another made-for-TV movie, but it helped to inspire the TV series that featured Kolchak fighting monsters, zombies and other creatures of the night. While the quality of the series never came close to equaling the strengths of these two movies, it helped Darren McGavin strike gold near the end of his career, playing a lovable curmudgeon and down-on-his-luck newspaper reporter that audiences saw as the definitive underdog.

While Dan Curtis used the veteran director John Moxey for *The Night Stalker*, he himself directed *The Night Strangler*, but the differences in directorial style are hardly noticeable, as the movies complement one another quite perfectly in both style and casting. In the original Curtis hired old vets Ralph Meeker, Claude Akins, Charles McGraw, Kent Smith and Elishu Cook, Jr. for supporting roles. In the sequel he employed John Carradine, Wally Cox and Margaret Hamilton. As mentioned, the Richard Matheson screenplays follow the same patterns. And the basic look of both films is similar, placing Gothic monsters, demons from the past, in glitzy urban settings.

Gary J. Svehla

The Mad Monster
PRC, 1942; Director: Sam Newfield

Jumping onto Universal's successful *The Wolf Man* bandwagon, PRC knocked out its own Wolf Man movie in five days. Starring as a mad scientist, George Zucco (who else) injects wolf blood into his hulking, childlike handyman Pedro (Glenn Strange, making his horror debut), changing the unfortunate simpleton into a dungaree-clad werewolf. Zucco expounds his improbable theories, the product of his demented brain, to a ghostly group of professors. He theorizes that by creating a race of wolf men with a lust to kill and with no thought for their personal safety, he can use them against the enemy and boost America's war effort. Give Sam Newfield his due, Strange transforms into the wolf man in just under five minutes. Normally in these efforts we have to wait a hell of a lot longer, and that includes Universal's Wolf Man opus. However, Strange's portrayal of Pedro makes Lon Chaney, Jr.'s performance as Lawrence Talbot in *The Wolf Man* appear like Laurence Olivier in a Shakespearean play. Mumbling lines of the caliber of "Did I walk in my sleep again?" when he changes from werewolf to man, Strange's drawling impersonation of an eight-year-old in a giant's body isn't very convincing, not all that far off the "talents" displayed by Tor Johnson in Ed Wood's oeuvre (and both actors were, ironically, ex-wrestlers). And *why* does every heroine in these 1930s and 1940s horror flicks have a boyfriend who just happens to be a snooping reporter that smells a rat, in this case Anne Nagel's father, Zucco. As usual, the police are shown to be a bunch of incompetents, as Strange murders a little girl, kills two of Zucco's disbelieving associates and prowls backward and forward through misty woods (in the same old spot, over and over again) without anybody catching him. Zucco, like Karloff and especially Lugosi, keeps the werewolf in check with that standard prop in 1940s horror flicks, a whip. It's not often you see a man change into a werewolf wearing a battered old hat, but you do in this one! Quibbles aside, *The Mad Monster* is actually pretty amusing fare if you are a die-hard fan of low-budget 1940s horror, with the customary conflagration at the end as Strange strangles Zucco and perishes in his burning house. The film received a 10-year ban in the U.K., as the censor felt that the public would be put off having blood transfusions, after seeing the movie, and it was eventually released in 1952, X-rated, with a disclaimer added that animal blood was *never* used in transfusions, so the British public could all rest easy in their beds at night.

Barry Atkinson

Lon Chaney, Jr. as Dan McCormick and Lionel Atwill as mad doctor Rigas

Man Made Monster
Universal, 1941; Director: George Waggner

Following his success as Lennie in *Of Mice and Men*, Universal began to promote the dubious talents of Lon Chaney, Jr., above Karloff and Lugosi, who were originally due to star in this picture. Although Chaney, Jr. was no great shakes as an actor, it was his name, and his father's reputation as a silent horror star, that the company was banking on to pull in the crowds. A rip-off of Karloff's 1936 *The Invisible Ray*, Chaney's first horror vehicle benefited from Elwood Bredell's superb black and white photography, fast-paced direction from Waggner and Hans J. Salter's bombastic, symphonic score (Salter was a superbly imaginative composer, never given his due in the higher echelons of Hollywood). Bulky Chaney, Jr. played Dan McCormick, a carnival act with an immunity to high doses of electricity—the Electrical Man—who is the sole survivor of a crash in which a bus ploughs into an electricity pylon. Taken to Dr. Samuel S. Hinds' house, the friendly-but-dim Chaney, Jr. falls into the hands of mad electro-biologist Lionel Atwill, who has plans afoot to create a race of super zombies that can survive on electricity alone. As the crazed Atwill subjects Chaney to ever-increasing doses of electrical current to prove his theories, Waggner and Bredell orchestrate the laboratory scenes with a series of quick cuts of flashing lights, electrical bolts, humming machinery, spinning dials, Atwill's leering face and Chaney, Jr.'s bemused expression, adding up to a wonderful montage of 1940s horror/sci-fi gone berserk! Eventually, Chaney, Jr. turns all melancholy, his drained strength now solely reliant on repeated quantities of electricity. The poor sap even gives up playing with Corky the dog (which means the audience doesn't have to suffer Salter's rather twee musical leitmotif when the terrier appears on screen). Encased in a rubber suit with a glowing head and hands, Chaney, under Atwill's hypnotic instructions, then murders kindly Hinds (who objects to Atwill's experimentation on the carnival performer) and is sent to the electric chair. But, his strength increases as he feeds off the massive current, he breaks out of the penitentiary and goes on a rampage, finishing off Atwill who, ironically, is electrocuted when he grabs hold of a metal door handle held by Chaney, Jr. Lumbering off with Hinds' niece, Anne Nagel, in his arms, Chaney, chased by the police and Corky, gets tangled up on a barbed wire fence, which rips open his rubber suit, the electricity drains from his body along the wire and leaves him a shrivelled corpse. Corky, in true doggy fashion, trots over and licks his dead face. Jack Pierce's makeup on Chaney (in the second part of the movie, he sports wrinkled, lined features) was considered by Universal to be insufficiently frightening, although John P. Fulton's effects of the monster stomping around with a pulsating, glowing head drew praise; nevertheless, *Man Made Monster* is full-blooded 1940s horror fodder and established Chaney as the new horror star of the decade, although, as mentioned, he was never in the same league as Karloff or even Lugosi in his prime.

Barry Atkinson

The Man Who Could Cheat Death
Hammer/Paramount, 1959; Director: Terence Fisher

At a period when Hammer Films was at the top of their game, undisputed classics such as *The Quatermass X-periment*, *Dracula*, *The Curse of Frankenstein* and *The Revenge of Frankenstein* already under their belts, with the likes of *The Mummy* and *The Brides of Dracula* waiting in the wings, it is very easy to overlook Terence Fisher's *The Man Who Could Cheat Death.* Is it because Anton Diffring (soon to star in the exploitive horror hit *Circus of Horrors*) was the main star and not Hammer stalwarts Peter Cushing and Christopher Lee (Lee was in it, but had an unsympathetic, almost minor, role as a doctor)? More talkative and less in the way of full-blooded mayhem may account for its cool reception with fans, as it had no vampires, mummies or a Frankenstein Monster for audiences to identify with. Whatever the reason, this story of a century-old doctor-cum-sculptor, who has discovered the secret of eternal youth by stealing glands from unwilling donors, is a well-mounted production from this fertile period in Hammer's history, photographed in rich Technicolor, although it never achieved the success it might have. The action takes place at the time of Diffring's next transplant. The doctor has to keep drinking a potion to impede the aging process, until the glands are procured (by murder, naturally), causing him to glow with a greenish light and burn anyone he comes into contact with. Lee, hopelessly infatuated with Hazel Court, who models for Diffring (who is also in love with her), is coerced into performing the operation after the doctor murders his long-time colleague and confidante, Arnold Marle, in a fit of temper. However, when Lee discovers the secret of Diffring's experiments keeping him forever youthful, he pretends that he has transplanted the glands when, in fact, he hasn't. The grisly climax sees Diffring aging rapidly to 104 years, all of his ills and diseases catching up with him. A terrified Court escapes from the inferno, started by the deranged, scarred doctor, who decays and goes up in flames. Apparently, the company was less than satisfied with Roy Ashton's makeup job on Diffring, as he quickly crumbles into a leprous monster, the general opinion being that it wasn't horrific enough and the scene itself too short. None of the sex scenes included in the accompanying novel appeared in the film either. But this lurid horror melodrama still puts many of Hammer's output of the 1960s firmly in the shade, and Diffring, in typical eye-rolling fashion, plays the crazed doctor with aplomb.

Barry Atkinson

The Man Who Lived Again
aka The Man Who Changed His Mind
Gaumont British, 1936; Director: Robert Stevenson

Boris Karloff, in one of his first mad doctor performances as Dr. Laurience (perhaps *The Invisible Ray* a year earlier started the trend), portrays a solitary scientist working on a contraption that switches brains electronically from one person to another (no gloppy brains in beakers or the use of scalpel or brain surgery required), much as we might transfer data from our computer's hard drive to a backup drive. While the tone of this stodgy Brit production (directed by Robert Stevenson) works against itself at times, Boris Karloff submits one of his best performances ever as a mad doctor. Sporting a full head of graying hair with a slightly stooped posture—always holding, sucking on or lighting a cigarette—a world-weary look of defeat always stamped on his face, Dr. Laurience surprisingly, especially for the time, invites a female scientist to join him in his research and medical experimentation, because she is the only colleague open to new ideas.

After working solo in a dilapidated lab, Laurience is seduced by the offer of corporate sponsorship by journalist Lord Haselwood (Frank Cellier), who offers Laurience richer quarters for his research and whose son Dick is making a play for Laurience's female assistant, Clare (Anna Lee). Haselwood rushes things and forces Laurience to publish his research and present his radical medical research to a public audience that verbally mocks the recluse. Of course this public ridicule is the impetus needed to drive Laurinece off the deep end, causing him to switch Lord Haselwood's brain with his patient/servant Clayton (Donald Calthrop), who earlier told Clare that he doesn't know what was worse, his miserable body or his perverted mind (the man is wheelchair bound, obviously a stroke victim with one side of his body partially paralyzed). Clayton's body dies during the experiment but not before laughing at the suggestion that Clayton makes, now in the seemingly fit body of Haselwood, that he at last inhabits a healthy body. In an ironic twist it is revealed that Haselwood is dying of heart disease, and that Clayton's brain has literally jumped from the fat into the fire.

By the time of the chilling climax, Laurience, in wild-eyed abandonment (with shadowy photography emphasizing the lisping delivery of dialogue), strangles the body of Lord Haselwood and makes sure he is seen by both servant and policeman leaving the Haselwood home, guaranteeing Laurience will be convicted of the journalist's murder. Laurience's scheme, in the meanwhile, is to switch his brain into Dick Haselwood's body, and switch Dick's brain into his own body, so Dick (in Laurience's body) will be executed for the murder of his father and Laurience (in Dick's body) will inherit Lord Haselwood's estate and fortune. In a weirdly imaginative performance during the climax, John Loder as Dick actually tries to imitate Karloff's Laurience, emphasizing his clenched hand holding a cigarette, his stiff gait and all Karloff's gestures observed earlier in the film.

After a terrifying fall from the second floor window, the body of Laurience lies dying on the ground, but Clare is able to undo the brain switching experiment, thus returning Dick to Dick's body and Laurience to Laurience's body, just before the evil scientist dies, recanting his research and ordering his lab destroyed by Clare.

The Man Who Lived Again lacks the twisted and audacious shenanigans inherent in most of the Monogram, PRC and Columbia mad doc films featuring Karloff or Bela Lugosi, but Karloff's performance is nuanced and rises above the film's other limitations. Seldom seen, classic horror buffs may be inclined to over praise the production, but while the film is at best of journeyman quality, Karloff's performance makes *The Man Who Lived Again* one film worth returning to time and time again.

Gary J. Svehla

The Man With Nine Lives
Columbia, 1940; Director: Nick Grinde

When it comes to Columbia's treasured "mad doctor" series, most consider either *The Devil Commands* or *The Man With Nine Lives* to be the best in series. Myself, I think *The Devil Commands* is the superior of the four entries, although *The Man With Nine Lives* is still entertaining, featuring a strong performance by Boris Karloff.

In *The Man With Nine Lives* Boris Karloff portrays Dr. Kravaal, a researcher working on a theory that freeze therapy may be a cure for cancer. Kravaal is eventually discovered frozen in ice 10 years after his disappearance. The film opens in an operating theater where Dr. Mason (Roger Pryor) demonstrates surgery based upon the work of Dr. Kravaal. Then the film switches locations and moves to the Canadian border cabin in Silverlake, where Kravaal disappeared. The rest of the film remains not only at the cabin, but for the most part in the basement of that cabin that contains two ice chambers. The film suffers from such a claustrophobic setting. Karloff's Kravaal is sympathetic but one note. He is working to save the life of a patient that he froze, and the man's nephew, along with the law, accuse the scientist of murder and order his arrest. Using poison gas Kravaal tries to overcome his mob-like jury and executioners, but all are trapped inside an ice cavern and frozen into a sort of suspended animation. Ironically, the patient survives but dies because he was left unattended in the outer room. Ten years pass and Dr. Mason and his romantic interest, also his nurse (Jo Ann Sayers), thaw out the doctor and his accusers. It seems the poison concoction allowed the group to be frozen and returned to life after being thawed, but the irate nephew destroys Kravaal's formula by throwing the paper into the fire. Kravaal shoots and kills the idiot. However, hoping to replicate the formula, Kravaal uses the human guinea pigs as test cases, but they all die. Last but not least, Mason and his nurse become the final guinea pigs to be tested.

Karloff's character of Kravaal morphs from sympathetic experimenter to obsessed and half-crazed scientist, who is willing to sacrifice the lives of humans for the cause of science. Karloff's character changes in *The Devil Commands* were more pronounced and interesting. He even altered his hairdo to illustrate the extent of his change. *The Devil Commands*, occurring mostly in his haunted country estate, did not feel so confining as the barebones *The Man With Nine Lives*. The character interaction in *The Man With Nine Lives* is not well

Roger Pryor, Boris Karloff and Jo Ann Sayers from *The Man With Nine Lives*

defined, with most of the characters becoming stereotypes of one kind or another. We have the good-hearted nurse, the kind doctor, the obsessed/insane doctor, the sheriff, the irate nephew, all of whom are in conflict. Nowhere is there to be found the brain-damaged buffoon of *The Devil Commands*, the evil spiritualist played by Anne Revere or any of the interesting off-kiltered characters from that production. When it comes to moody cinematography, *The Devil Commands* features a haunted mansion with shadowy entrances and exits, and a crazy laboratory filled with corpses wearing metallic headgear. It's simply a more outrageous production. *The Man With Nine Lives* features mountain cabins and ice chambers and lacks the iconic horror aspects to make it a memorable or stand out production.

Bottom line, *The Man With Nine Lives* is a solid B programmer with an interesting Boris Karloff performance and a novel plot involving cryogenics. This film appeared a generation before reports surfaced that Walt Disney was frozen at the time of his death. Both it and *The Devil Commands* are superior to the other two productions in the "Mad Doctor" series, but *The Devil Commands* still remains the superior entry. For all fans of classic horror, *The Man With Nine Lives* is a blessing nonetheless.

Gary J. Svehla

Mill of the Stone Women
Galatea Film/Parade Releasing , 1960; Director: Giorgio Ferroni

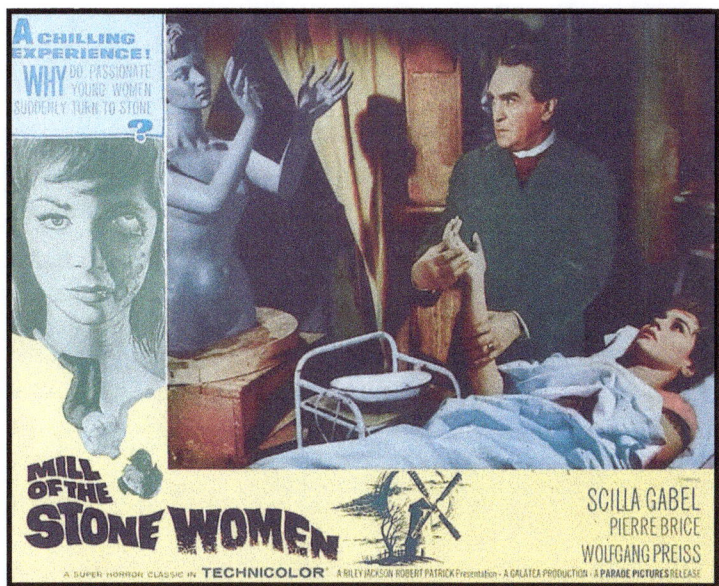
Wolfgang Preiss looks at the stone statue of a former patient

A beautifully photographed (in inky blues and grays, with rich mauves) continental horror melodrama that was a direct successor, in some ways, to Ricardo Freda's *Lust of the Vampire* (*I Vampiri*) in its tale of a young girl suffering from a life-threatening blood disease, who needs constant transfusions to keep her alive. Wolfgang Preiss (giving a fine impersonation of Bela Lugosi) is her professor father who, with the aid of his criminal assistant, a doctor, kidnaps young women, drains them of their blood to give to his daughter and turns the corpses into stone, sculpting the bodies and exhibiting them as statues of notorious women on his renowned carousel. The year is 1912 and a young student, Pierre Brice, arrives at the gloomy old windmill to write a thesis on the 100-year-old carousel, housed within the windmill, but he soon finds himself drawn inexorably to a strange girl (Scilla Gabel) seen wandering around, despite Preiss warning him to stay away from her. The windmill itself resembles a Gothic edifice—a fantastically constructed maze of timbers and rafters with cramped, interconnecting rooms that are cluttered with cobwebby junk, the windmill's machinery and models of body parts laying in the shadows. Preiss' laboratory is situated in the bowels of the windmill; some of the more explicit shots of the actor surrounded by the naked corpses of women were cut from U.S. and U.K. prints. As Gabel becomes ill, her radiant features deteriorate into a haggard, blemished mask, only reverting back to normal after she has been given a fresh supply of new blood. Finally, the doctor creates a serum that, when mixed with blood, will restore the professor's daughter permanently, but there is a price—he wants to marry Gabel after the operation. The professor's emphatic answer is "No." In the frenetic climax, Preiss attempts to use Brice's girlfriend as an unwilling donor, but the vial of precious serum is smashed when the professor stabs the doctor to death. Unable to perform the life-saving transfusion, a deranged Preiss sets fire to the windmill and both he and his dying, emaciated daughter perish in the blaze, as the student and his girl escape. The final nightmarish scenes show the wax melting off the petrified corpses on the carousel, revealing the blackened skulls. Released in Britain and parts of Europe as *Drops of Blood*, this handsome-looking French/Italian horror film, containing an eerie score by Carlo Innocenzi, was unashamedly modeled on the Hammer output of the time (the movie is dedicated to Terence Fisher) and is a fine reminder of continental fantasy cinema at its most evocative.

Barry Atkinson

Metropolis
UFA; Paramount 1927; Director: Fritz Lang

Other than *Nosferatu*, Fritz Lang's *Metropolis* is perhaps the most groundbreaking film of German cinema, and even when viewing an incomplete, restored version of a classic originally released in 1927, the film's audacity and creativity continues to shine through. Visually, the film is just as mesmerizing today as it was to silent film audiences 80 years ago. Just the symbolism of watching Freder (Gustav Frohlich) replace the underground worker at the clock, each human slave required to move the huge metal hands of the clock to the positions marked by ever-changing lit light

bulbs, working such an arduous task without break for 10 hour shifts, summarizes the plight of the oppressed working-class population. The movie's major theme, spelled out boldly throughout the film, is that *head* and *hands* need a *mediator*—the heart. In other words the aboveground idea men, the planners, the upper class, need the sweat and toil of the belowground working class to make their ideas reality. As the movie opens, the relationship between those above ground and those below is one of oppression and the rich getting richer and the poor getting the shaft while down there. Enter an underground prophet Maria (Brigitte Helm), an innocent and hauntingly beautiful woman, who preaches in front of a huge candle-lit underground altar, with several Christian crosses framing her. She preaches that a Mediator will arise and bring the "head" and "arms" together in "love." So when corporate supreme leader Joh Fredersen (Alfred Abel) gets wind of the potential rebellion, he turns to the mad inventor Rotwang (Rudolf Klein-Rogge) to use his alchemy to turn the workers against Maria.

First of all, the chemistry between Rotwang and Fredersen is interesting. In his medieval-looking home, standing right in the center of the futuristic city of Metropolis, Rotwang houses a shrine to his past, sequestered behind curtains. It is a large bust of Hel, the woman he loved most in the world, and the woman that married Fredersen and died while giving birth to his son Freder, the same young man who sneaks to the world below the surface to find Maria, a woman he gazed upon only once, but once was enough to fall deeply in love. Fredersen feels Rotwang is on his side, or at least on the side of the aboveground upper-class society. But Rotwang harbors lustful feelings for Maria and continues to hate Fredersen. Showing Fredersen his mad laboratory, an iconic one with bubbling beakers with flowing liquids, electronic gizmos and pipes of fluids passing from one container to another, proudly Rotwang displays his mechanic woman, a fabulous robot with expressionless facial features, two breasts and a slender feminine frame. Glistening in metallic sheen, the robot is able to be transformed into human flesh and blood, duplicating any human being who is wired to Rotwang's transfer tunnel machine. In a scary sequence Maria, alone underground, walks away from her altar in the cavernous stone beehive below and is startled by strange sounds. A light from a flashlight shines above and below her, and it suddenly appears at her feet, and soon the light shines on her face, as Rotwang leers at the defenseless beauty. Once she falls unconscious, Rotwang, in a stance similar to the gorilla that carried its female victim across rooftops in *Murders in the Rue Morgue*, carries his victim back to his lab. There she is placed totally naked in his transference tunnel (metal strips block strategic areas of anatomy) and the metal mechanical woman becomes an exact copy of Maria, except that Rotwang controls her thoughts. After the transformation, actress Brigitte Helm wears heavier eye makeup and changes her facial expressions from innocent to sinister. She assumes Maria's role as preacher, but instead of speaking of peace and the Mediator coming, she now speaks of uprisings and the destruction of the major machines.

Rotwang's image of mad scientist became the template for those who followed. Rotwang sports an artificial metal hand, covered by a glove, and sports wild and frizzy white hair. Although he is a little squat and on the short side, he is apt to suffer fits of rage, hopping around, his hands and arms flailing and his manic eyes wide open in wonderment and rage. In his evil lab, he is the master of his domain, displaying proudly the technological wonders that make him superior, at least in his own mind. When he shows leader Fredersen his robot, seated stiffly and staring blankly ahead, it is with total arrogance that he presents to Fredersen this tribute to Hel. For Fredersen is the man Rotwang hates for marrying Hel, for impregnating her and for watching her die giving birth to his son Freder. A more insane, obsessive ranting and raving maniac could not be found. Rotwang—the predator, preying on the young and innocent Maria, allowing his genius to be used for evil intent—becomes one of the most classic mad doctors in movie history.

Gary J. Svehla

Mimic
Dimension, 1997; Director: Guillermo del Toro

Breaking taboos (savagely slaughtering innocent children) and watching expensive shots of exploding underground tunnel and train setpieces no longer does it for me. *Mimic*, directed by gifted Mexican director Guillermo Del Toro, is better than average horror fare, and to be honest, the film's first half is moodily impressive. The opening shots of the dying children in hospital beds are intense. And the shots of the bugs—disguised as homeless people—are eerie. My favorite sequence is the bug/person who invades the laboratory at night, and, while its presence is felt in every shadow, its appearance is never viewed outright. Terrifying and unpleasant at the same time, the film is at its best in moments such as these. Also gripping is the sequence where the autistic child enters the "hive," now occupying a deserted mission in the middle of the poor side of town. His innocence, fearlessness and uncanny ability to mimic the insect sounds makes the boy seem like a conduit between the insect and human world. These sequences, all in the first half, promise something quite horrific and mood evoking. But unfortunately, the film's second half plays things too safe and mines the past instead of plowing the future.

For in the film's second half we meet *Aliens* revisited, this time with a giant Bug King (instead of the Alien Queen) that is protecting the hive's eggs. The eerie attacks underground and on the train are nicely rendered and do arouse the emotions, but the film's finale, where the hero, who has sacrificed himself to save humankind, finds himself suddenly rescued, smacks of a sequel. And the fact that he is probably no longer a human but now "one of them" is painfully obvious as he walks very bug-like up the long steps, wearing a shape-disguising blanket.

Okay at best, but the film's derivative plot ruins directorial inspirations.

The mad scientist turns out to be humanitarian entomologist, Susan Tyler (Mira Sorvino), who engineers a mutant breed of insect designed to kill disease-carrying cockroaches. Supposed to die out after one generation, the genetically created super bugs decide to take over the human race instead, proving that in horror films things never work out as planned and never try to play God.

Gary J. Svehla

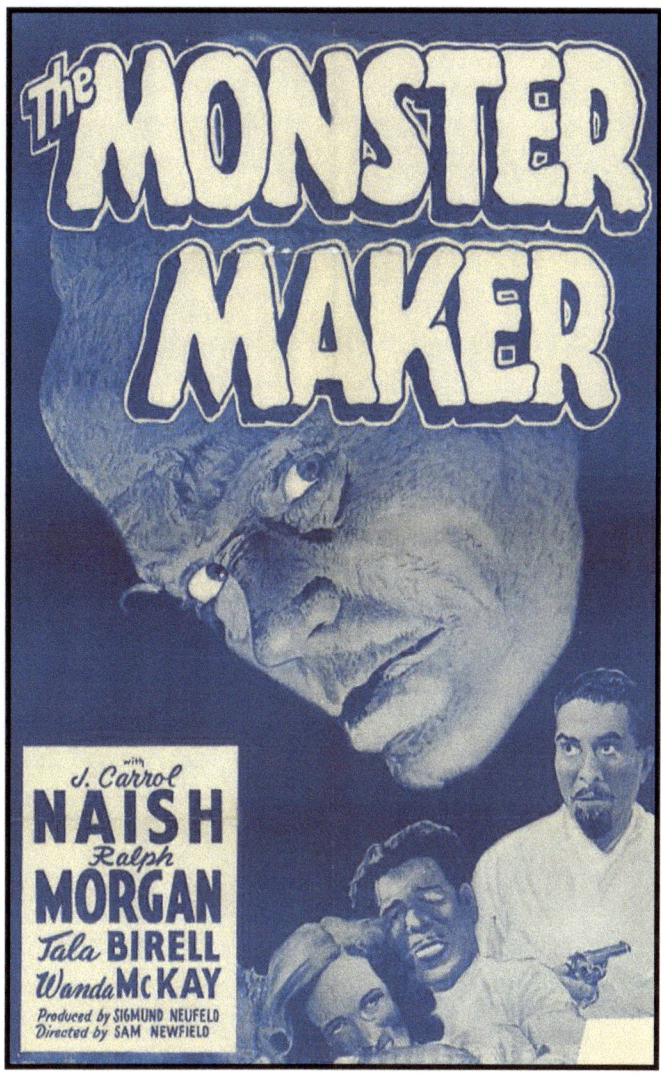

The Monster Maker
PRC, 1944; Director: Sam Newfield

PRC was a Poverty Row studio producing, in tandem with other major studios such as Universal, a string of horror films during the 1940s, produced mostly with the same set-up of stars and crew (a Poverty Row repertory company). *The Monster Maker* was one of its better efforts, a grim little tale concerning the effects of the distorting disease of acromegaly on the human pituitary gland. J. Carrol Naish played the evil Dr. Igor Markoff. In an elaborate plot, Naish escapes from Europe with his female assistant after injecting his unfaithful wife with acromegaly bacteria and murdering her doctor lover. He takes on his rival's identity and steals his ideas to gain notoriety. At a concert, Naish's doctor becomes besotted to the point of obsession with blonde Wanda McKay, whose father (Ralph Morgan) is a famed pianist. McKay resembles his dead wife and Naish refuses to leave her alone, even though she's engaged. In a confrontation between Naish and Morgan, who has visited the doctor to warn him off his daughter, the pianist is walloped over the head and injected with acromegaly germs. Four weeks later, Morgan has become horribly deformed, his swollen hands unable to hit the piano keys and his features so ghastly that he locks himself away in a darkened room to avoid all human contact. The twist here is that Naish is the only person that has the necessary antidote to cure him and he will—on one condition—instruct his daughter to accept his hand in marriage. Eventually manacled to a bed in Naish's house by henchman Glenn Strange (soon to take on the Frankenstein monster role in *House of Frankenstein*), Morgan breaks free of his bonds, shoots Naish dead and is cured by the doctor's sympathetic assistant. He's back playing the piano again in the final reel. Newfield directs in leisurely style, almost like a stage play and a bit sluggishly at times. Albert Glasser contributes one of his earlier scores to a well-acted and well-scripted drama that also contains a first-rate make-up job on Morgan, as the pianist with the misshapen features. And there is the obligatory giant ape housed in Naish's laboratory. It doesn't do a great deal, but an awful lot of 1940s horror movies had to include one, and *The Monster Maker* was no exception!

Barry Atkinson

Monster on the Campus
Universal, 1958; Director: Jack Arnold

Jack Arnold's final science fiction/horror movie for Universal turned out to be (rather surprisingly, given the director's reputation) a flatly directed effort with a less-than-sparkling script, lacking the keen edge that turned his previous features into minor classics. The familiar man-into-ape format had doctor Arthur Franz importing a coelacanth from Madagascar to use as a lesson for his college students. Unfortunately, the fish is radioactive, and any ingestion of its fluids regresses the person or animal back to a primitive state, in Franz's case a murderous Neanderthal-type monster. First to "change" is Troy Donahue's Alsatian hound, lapping up the fish's fluids and growing long fangs, acting like a savage beast. Next is a dragonfly, sucking on the fish and developing a two-foot wingspan, buzzing around Franz's laboratory like a model airplane. Then it's the turn of Franz himself, cutting his hand on the coelacanth's teeth and even smoking his pipe after radioactive fluid has dripped into the tobacco! It all sounds far-fetched and you get the distinct impression that Arnold had a lot less empathy with this material than he did with, say, *Creature from the Black Lagoon* or *The Incredible Shrinking Man*. Nevertheless, the director does show flashes of his undoubted skill by conjuring up some grimly horrific moments such as, the corpse of Franz's female assistant, tied to a tree by her hair, dead eyes staring blankly into the night; the monster's shadow on the street edging slowly toward a police officer on the telephone; a hairy claw appearing through a half-open door; and Franz transforming into the ferocious ape-like creature, smashing up a room rigged with camera and recording equipment, in uncomprehending fury. Franz is finally shot dead by police after abducting his girlfriend, Joanna Moore, and changing into the monster right in front of their disbelieving eyes. Workmanlike to say the least, Universal even tagged on the main theme to *Tarantula* over the title credits to save the expense of writing a new score, a money-saving idea that did little to enhance a rather predictable effort from the company, becoming Arnold's least-rewarding horror film.

Barry Atkinson

Orloff and The Invisible Man
Celia, 1971; Director: Pierre Chevalier

In this 1971 release directed by Pierre Chevalier, the always-reliable Howard Vernon brings his original Dr. Orloff character out of retirement, in this sleazy, almost soft-core horror thriller that borrows from everyone.

The movie begins as a Hammer clone with Dr. Garondet (Francis Valladares) summoned to the castle of Orloff. When he sstops first at the tavern overlooking the castle, everyone grunts, looks uneasily at one another and disappear into the woodwork. We actually expect to see Michael Ripper toss the poor doctor out of the establishment. One hard-up bastard accepts the doctor's offer of money for a ride, but the carriage only goes so far before it gets stuck. When the carriage driver orders the doctor to get out and push, the carriage drives away and the doctor is forced to walk the remaining distance.

Arriving at the castle, Garondet is greeted by both the silently passive daughter of Orloff and ugly, cruel servants before finally meeting the even more mysterious Professor Orloff himself, who has created an invisible monster, the sight of which is mind-blowing to behold. The monster, in actuality a man in a cheap gorilla outfit, becomes visibly transparent as he threatens both male and female alike.

Orloff and the Invisible Man is one bad movie, but nevertheless, an interesting one with a sense of drama, mood and style.

Gary J. Svehla

The Raven
Universal, 1935; Director: Louis Friedlander/Lew Landers

The Raven is an often-underrated 1935 movie directed by Lew Landers. Of all the Karloff and Lugosi Universal entries, *The Raven* is the only one that features Lugosi in a

role that overshadows Karloff's performance. And Lugosi's portrayal of Dr. Vollin is in many ways his best performance in a non-character role (i.e., Ygor or Dracula). Never has Lugosi looked more handsome or distinguished, and his line delivery is much more natural than it was in *Dracula*. His demented personality housing both the distinguished surgeon and the depraved psychopath has never been better displayed. *The Raven* offers a *tour de force* performance by Bela Lugosi. And Lugosi's progression into lunacy is amazing. We first meet him when Judge Thatcher (Samuel S. Hines) implores the now retired surgeon to operate on his daughter Jean (Irene Ware), to save her life. The doctor is firm in his refusal until Thatcher admits the other surgeons stated that Vollin would be the best man for the job, and then his overblown ego kicks in and he agrees to operate. The grateful and fully recovered Jean repeatedly thanks Vollin and dedicates her new dance recital (she is a professional dancer) to Edgar Allan Poe, Vollin's idol. But when Jean mentions her fiancé, the sexually obsessed surgeon shows his true colors and makes it known he expects the young girl to thank him in the marriage bed. Vollin will settle for no less.

Vollin invites the Judge, Jean and her fiancé (Lester Matthews) to his home for a dinner party, with a few other guests in attendance. The house, ornate and opulent in its excess, is revealed to have secret passageways, rooms that move up and down from level to level, torture chambers in the cellar, etc. Before long the Judge is shackled to a slab with a pendulum blade swinging closer and closer to his heart, while Jean is kidnapped. In a splendid over-the-top performance, Vollin states torturing others is the only cure for the mental torture he faces in losing the love of his life to another man. In wonderful sequences, Lugosi flails his arms and shakes them about, cackles like a madman, throws his hands over his eyes and falls forward, landing fast and hard on his knees. His is a physical and eccentric performance that simply works in his outrageousness and clearly exemplifies why Bela Lugosi is such a cherished horror film personality.

Karloff as Bateman, a rough and tumble gangster in need of a new face fast, is best in his initial sequences when he pleads for Vollin to help him, even at the point of a gun. And after the operation is finished, the safely protected Vollin, looking at and speaking to Bateman through a grille in the ceiling, demands that Bateman become his servant in order for him to fix his paralyzed face. Unfortunately, for the rest of the movie, Karloff does little more than obey the beck and call of Vollin. *The Raven* is truly Bela Lugosi's movie, and in it he demonstrates flashes of the romantic leading man that he so wanted to become. But for horror genre fans, we gravitate toward Lugosi's mental extremes and physical meltdowns, so marvelously crafted.

Gary J. Svehla

Return of the Fly
20th Century Fox, 1959; Director: Edward L. Bernds

Fox rushed out this sequel to cash in on the enormous and totally unexpected success of *The Fly,* but it's a better follow-up than usual, a well-made, capable horror yarn boosted by the presence of Vincent Price and a fine soundtrack by Paul Sawtell. Although not in color, CinemaScope photography was employed, a real bonus for horror fans in the 1950s. Years after his father's hushed-up death, young Brett Halsey, against uncle Vincent Price's wishes, wants to continue with the disintegrater/integrater program and cajoles the unwilling Price into financing the project, setting up his laboratory in his grandfather's mansion. Unfortunately, Halsey's partner (a smarmy David Frankham) happens to be a criminal on the run, a weasel who is stealing his boss's secrets and collaborating with another slimy villain, who runs a funeral parlor, agreeing to a 50/50 split on any cash that they make by selling the blueprints of the transmitting machines to the highest bidder. The first piece of monster mayhem, after the

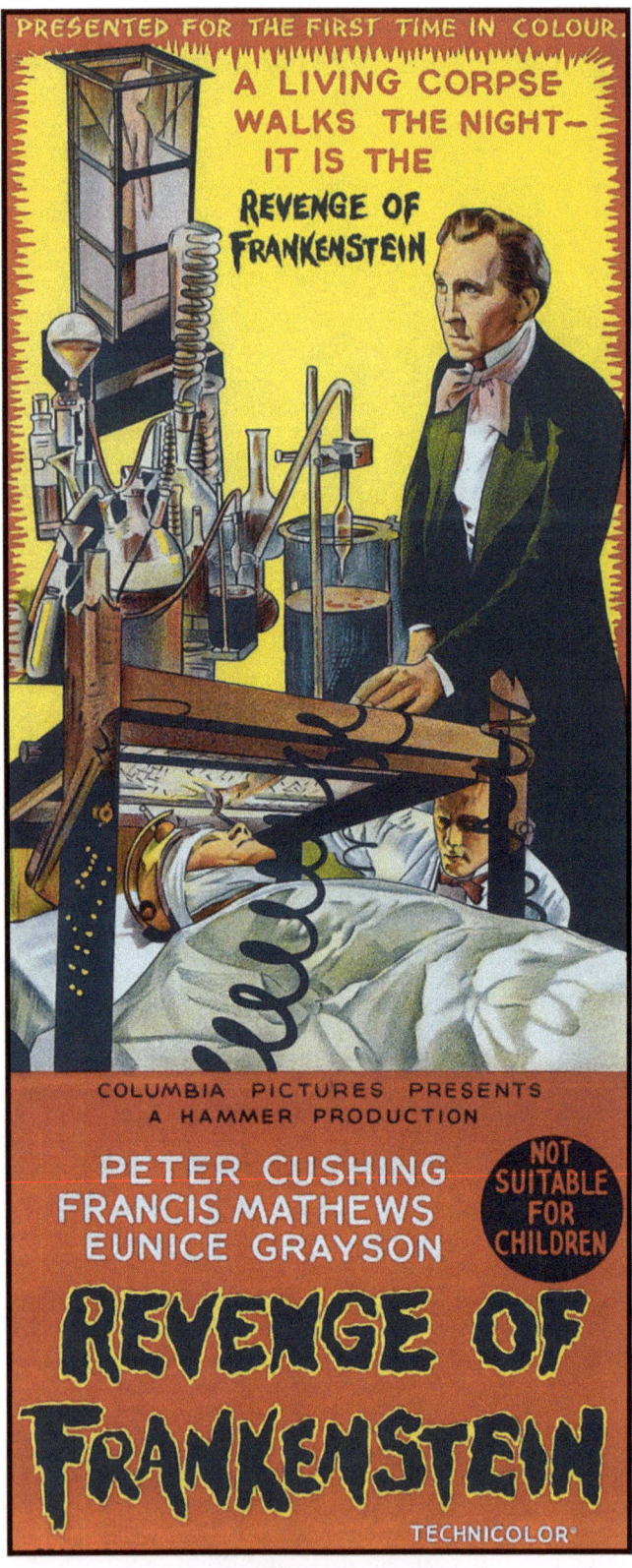

crossing him and they fight; Halsey is knocked unconscious and bundled into one of the machines with a fly (understandably, he has a morbid fear of the insects). When a bewildered Price turns on the transmitter, his nephew reappears, sporting a huge fly's head, arm and leg. The picture then follows the customary formula of monster-on-the loose with police in hot pursuit, as Halsey stumbles around seeking revenge by,killing both criminals before returning to his laboratory and an unusually happy ending. He is placed in one of the transmitters with the fly-with-the-doctor's-head and emerges in one piece, much to the relief of his girlfriend and Price. There are a few eerie scenes of the fly-creature attacking the overweight criminal, among the coffins in the parlor, and the obligatory "shadow on the wall" shot as Halsey creeps around the mansion. The black and white CinemaScope photography is a winner as well, lending the production an extra sheen. Fox had one more stab at this story in 1965 with *Curse of the Fly*, but this turned out to be the most inferior of the original *Fly* trilogy.

Barry Atkinson

The Revenge of Frankenstein
Columbia, 1958; Director: Terence Fisher

Photographed in glorious inky Technicolor, Hammer's elegantly structured sequel to *The Curse of Frankenstein* remains one of the most intelligently handled of any *Frankenstein* movie, with Peter Cushing giving a superbly mannered performance as the Baron.

In his second *Frankenstein* outing, the Baron is more sympathetic than in the previous picture, with a hint of compassion, even though totally obsessed with creating the perfect human being. With the aid of his crippled, hunchbacked assistant Karl, he escapes the guillotine (an unfortunate priest is substituted), on condition that he gives the hunchback a new body. Cushing plays Doctor Victor Stein, who shuns the overtures of Carlsbruck's medical council, but he has most of the female population queuing in his waiting room to be checked over, while fluttering their eyelashes at him. Stein uses the patients in his hospital for the poor as a source of body parts for his new creation, which is secreted away in his marvelous period laboratory. Taking on young doctor Francis Mathews as a keen and willing assistant, Karl's brain is soon inside his new body (lanky, good-looking Michael Gwynn); locked in an attic after the operation, the new being breaks free of his room when he learns of Cushing's plans to have him exhibited as a medical attraction alongside his old body. In one of Hammer's most unforgettable (and key) sequences, a drunken and sadistic janitor beats Gwynn mercilessly, when the janitor discovers him in the act of destroying his former body; brain-damaged by his injuries, his dribbling features contorting with rage, he strangles the man and hides in the stables where, to his horror, his body begins to twist itself back into its old shape. After murdering a local girl, the tremendous climax sees Gwynn, now crazed and deformed, crashing through French windows into a society party and

rather tangled storyline has been established, is when a snoopy police inspector, on Frankham's trail, gets shoved into one of the transmitter machines and emerges from the other machine with the hands and feet of a guinea pig, dead. His suspicions aroused, Halsey discovers that his friend has been double-exposing Cushing as Frankenstein. The horrified gathering watches as the pathetic creature asks Frankenstein for help before he collapses into a misshapen heap. Cushing is then battered to death by his enraged hospital patients, but Mathews manages to place the Baron's brain into a new body (which just happens to look like Cushing!), and in London, Cushing resurfaces as Doctor Franck. He has, ironically, ended up as one of his own creations.

With a snappy script, decent acting by all concerned (especially Gwynn as the agonized Karl) and artful direction by Fisher, this handsome horror picture went further in establishing Hammer Films as one of Britain's foremost independent production companies, and the press at the time was now referring to Cushing as "the new Karloff," a label he became quite bemused with over the years.

Barry Atkinson

Sexy Irish McCalla poses in the left-side border, while in the mad lab Nazi war criminal Osler, played by Rudolph Anders, gets to work.

She Demons
Astor, 1958; Director: Richard E. Cunha

The second of Cunha's quartet of horror/fantasy movies, *She Demons,* released by Astor in 1958, even by the director's own cheapo standards, was the tackiest of the four, saddled with cardboard sets that in some scenes can be seen shaking. And check out those rocky walls. They resemble nothing more than screwed-up paper painted gray. *She Demons* creates a parody of Nazism at its most hilarious; dressed in Gestapo/stormtrooper outfits and ending every sentence with the shout of "Swine," a parade of B extras do a very bad impression of German brutality, worthy of a Christmas pantomime where the audience screams "Boo!" at every appearance of the villain. The movie's one saving grace is stunning blonde Irish McCalla, at the time a TV actress starring in *Sheena, Queen of the Jungle*. Her refined good looks and voluptuous figure probably had the cast and crew sweating under their collars during shooting, particularly near the beginning where she undresses beside a panting Tod Griffin. Anyway, back to the movie. Griffin, McCalla (a spoiled socialite), Victor Sen Yung and Charlie Opuni are shipwrecked on a volcanic island, where mad scientist and Nazi war criminal Rudolph Anders is trying to find a permanent solution to his once-beautiful wife's disfigured features, tapping into the island's lava and transferring the energy, with added radiation, to his laboratory. He names his discovery "Character X." He exchanges the radiation-treated genes from a bevy of lithesome women, kidnapped from a neighboring island to his wife but it has only a temporary effect. The victims' features take on the characteristics of his wife's scarred looks, leaving them with grotesque faces and exhibiting animal tendencies. The she-devils are kept in a cage after the operations, presided over by the stormtroopers. Anders captures the three castaways (Opuni is killed in the first reel) and sets his sights immediately on the ravishing but feisty McCalla, striking a deal; if she becomes his mistress, he will spare her from being the next subject on his operating table. Needless to say, she turns the oily German down (a juicy, lip-smacking piece of overacting from Anders), As the mad scientist prepares to operate, the Americans, using the island for target practice, bomb the island. The explosions then cause the volcano to erupt (cue for stock footage from *One Million B.C.*), Anders is buried under molten lava and his wife reveals part of her ravaged face before expiring, leaving Griffin, McCalla and Sen Young to escape. Okay, Cunha's schlock-effort doesn't drag over 77 minutes, and an ogle-worthy dance scene, performed by a group of scantily dressed native girls, occurs a third of the way in, but compared to his other three pictures, *She Demons* isn't very inventive, is woodenly acted (apart from Anders), seems rushed and plagiarizes an awful lot of similar films. The haughty McCalla is the one real reason to catch it!

Barry Atkinson

Shivers
aka They Came from Within
Trans American, 1975; Director: David Cronenberg

David Cronenberg was much more fun when he began his feature film career as a horror film director and made *Shivers* (retitled *They Came From Within* for U.S. release) in 1976. When released in the U.S., the MPAA forced the distributor to trim the release print to get an R rating, and so Americans never saw the uncut director's print of the movie until the movie was released to home DVD.

Right at the dawning of sexual conservatism, with the emergence of AIDS a few years off, blood-borne sexually

transmitted diseases slowly gained publicity. *Shivers* details the end of the Age of Aquarius and, with it, the sexually promiscuous lifestyles that promoted orgies, swinging and wife swapping. In this exploitative gem, a scientist uses a sexually active young woman to create a phallic (of course!) parasite that eliminates all sexual inhibitions. She infects several people living in a newly opened Canadian high-rise apartment complex, and for the rest of the movie, the sexual acrobatics between male and female (and female and female and male and male) escalate until the modern plague-infested victims finally hop into automobiles and threaten to infect all of Canada.

Of course this film depicts such an epidemic not as a softcore sex movie might, but as an exploitative horror movie 1970s-style did, with a male host existing in semi-zombie state throughout the movie, his phallic pet slithering out of his mouth and back in again, the parasite writhing slightly under the skin wiggling across his abdomen. Such sexual predators force themselves on unwary victims, climaxing by transferring the parasite from themselves to their newly initiated hosts, orally. Once infected, humans become zombified vessels for their parasite and resemble a product of the George Romero school of filmmaking. Even horror cult actress Barbara Steele has a cameo as Betts, a lesbian ready to exit her closet (or in this case, bathtub).

As seen today, *Shivers* has lost a lot of its edge and surprise; however, David Cronenberg's direction is still devilishly claustrophobic (getting the most out of his swinging apartment complex) and features shock upon shock, delivered in his typical gooey biological manner. Perennial Cronenberg actor Joe Silver delivers an effective supporting role, and heroine Lynn Lowry submits a heroin-chic performance that resembles the similar turn committed by Dana Wynter in the original *Invasion of the Body Snatchers*. Lowry seems to have been selected for her parasite-infected performance, which is outstanding, contrasted to her generic pretty heroine that any young actress could play.

In Cronenberg's world, the fine line between scientific progress and sexual promiscuity is erased, as the in-the-lab created organism gets totally, and rapidly, out of hand once it incites sexual libertarianism. Talk about the ultimate pandemic!

Gary J. Svehla

Tarantula
Universal, 1955; Director: Jack Arnold

Which was the better of these two 1950s giant-insect thrillers—*Them!* or *Tarantula*? Jack Arnold's movie wins by a whisker, I think. More "in-your-face" than the Warner Bros.' flick, with a tight plot; snappy script; decent, pared to the bone, acting; fantastic effects by Clifford Stine and a bombastic score by Henry Mancini, plus Arnold's favored location, the desert. These combined elements have made Universal's superior giant bug outing the archetypal monster

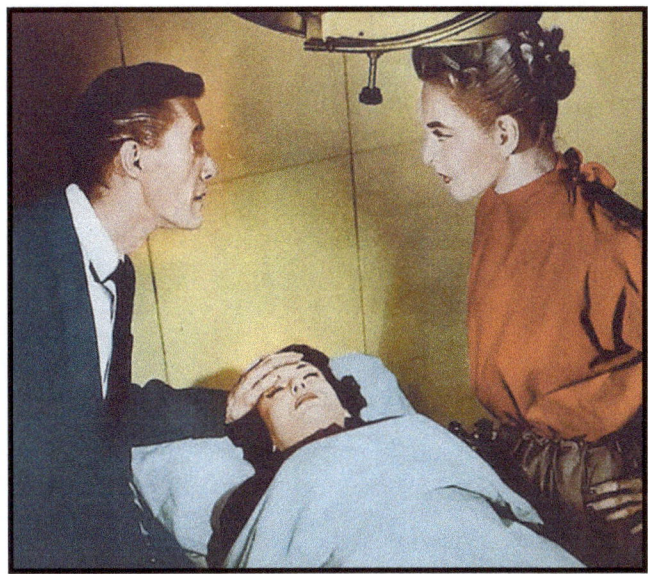

Dr. Charles Conway (John Carradine) turns beautiful women into mutants, in *The Unearthy*.

spider movie of them all. Roping in Leo G. Carroll to play a biologist, experimenting with a growth nutrient in his desert laboratory, was a good move. Carroll's low-key style gives the film its much-needed air of gravitas, amid all the theatrics, as the spider escapes from the lab and goes on a rampage. John Agar and Mara Corday blend perfectly as a couple of doctors, Corday stunning in a series of white outfits. The movie had two storylines running side-by-side—the effects of Carroll's nutrient on humans, resulting in the deformity caused by acromegaly, and of course, its effect on animals, causing them to grow at an alarming rate. Arnold's economical, no-nonsense direction produced some classic scenes of monster mayhem—the gigantic spider poised like a fearsome black statue above a ranch before crawling slowly down the slope toward its prey—a herd of horses; the monster approaching a window, as Corday undresses for bed, its multifaceted eyes staring at her through the glass; the tarantula smashing through electricity pylons and crushing to matchwood Carroll's house; and the giant spider appearing menacingly over the distant hillside as the town's citizens are placing explosives to stop the thing in its tracks. And let's not forget all those disfigured humans suffering from acromegaly, adding an extra dose of horror to the proceedings. *Tarantula*, from the first date of its release, ran non-stop for an incredible 15 years in Britain, a real crowd-grabber, double billed with other Universal favorites, a few Hammer features and Toho's *Rodan*, and is now highly regarded by buffs as a seminal monster movie, and one of Universal's best-ever horror features. Look out for Clint Eastwood, as one of the pilots dropping bombs on the tarantula in the closing minutes.

Barry Atkinson

The Unearthly
Republic/AB-PT Productions, 1957; Director: Brooke L. Peters

Owing a lot to United Artist's *The Black Sleep* for its ideas and contents, *The Unearthly* had the familiar plot of a mad scientist (John Carradine) trying to halt mankind's aging process by creating a new gland that, when transplanted into the body, will grant that person eternal youth. Unfortunately, the patients he has experimented on are transformed into hideous-looking mutants that are locked away in cellars beneath his mansion. To disguise his operations, Carradine pretends to be a doctor curing depressive illnesses, his patients never suspecting his true motives. Myron Healy, an undercover cop posing as a criminal, arrives at the mansion hoping to expose Carradine for what he really is. Healy is greeted at the door by lumbering, dimwitted Lobo, the scientist's henchman (Tor Johnson, as Lobo, also played "Lobo" in Ed Wood's *Bride of the Monster* and *Night of the Ghouls*. This must count as Johnson's most wooden of all wooden performances!), and the scientist, believing Healy to be a killer on the loose, says that he can stay on one condition, that he subjects himself to Carradine's glandular experiments. Sally Todd is Carradine's next victim, drugged by assistant Marylin Buferd, who loves her boss to bits (as do all female assistants in these movies; unrequited love, that is never returned). But eight hours after the operation, the attractive Todd is changed into a grotesque, disfigured monstrosity and Healy, coming across the poor girl

in an underground room, begins to smell a rat, warning Allison Hayes that she may be the next "patient" to fall into Carradine's trap. After Carradine attempts to imprison Healy and Hayes, the police arrive in the nick of time. Carradine is killed by one of his botched experiments, a brain-damaged zombie; the hulking Lobo is handcuffed as he hovers mournfully over Carradine's body; Hayes falls into Healy's arms and two cops discover a large cellar crammed full of deranged mutants, resembling the animal people in *Island of Lost Souls*. More 1940s in feel than a 1950s movie, *The Unearthly* is standard horror fare for the undiscriminating, enlivened by an over-the-top star turn from horror stalwart Carradine, who carries the day.

Barry Atkinson

The Vampire
United Artists, 1957: Director: Paul Landres

Producers Arthur Gardner and Jules V. Levy made what I consider the suburban Gothics, featuring mythic horror icons dressed up in all the accoutrements of 1950s Americana. *The Vampire*, written by Pat Fielder and directed by Paul Landres, is one of 1950s American B classics, right up there with the best of Toho, AIP, Allied Artists, Film Group and any of the Indies. *The Vampire* stars the mature, fatherly John Beal in a wonderful performance, but he lacked the youth appeal of other drive-in movie fare of this era. Movies such as *The Vampire* and *Return of Dracula* were not drive-in fodder, they were released directly to the neighborhood (suburban) theaters and appealed to more than merely the youth trade. Proudly considered a programmer, *The Vampire*'s crew had the ingenuity of vision and the creativity of set decoration, which makes the film stand out among inferior and more widely heralded productions that made more money. I was lucky enough to have seen this movie theatrically at age seven, and my love for the genre was sparked by this and other B romps.

The Vampire casts the mythic Euro-vampire in a bright new scientific sheen, filtered through shades of *Dr. Jekyll and Mr. Hyde*. Screenwriter Pat Fielder made sure she touched every one of the Gothic bases in small town America. The film establishes its suburban roots in the very first sequence, when a drugstore delivery boy on a bike drops off a prescription to Dr. Campbell, who lives and works in a typical large (but run down) suburban cottage. The boy finds the doctor near death and runs to fetch Dr. Beecher (John Beal), who hurries over to make a house call (something lost after the 1950s). With his dying breath, Campbell delivers a speech how his lifetime of experiments are contained within the pills he thrusts forth and which Beecher places in his lab coat pocket. Then Campbell dies. Returning to his suburban home/office (his daughter Betsy, Lydia Reed, dances ballet in a room directly outside the doctor's office), Beecher asks his daughter to get one of his migraine pills, and of course the adorable child reaches into the wrong pocket and produces the wrong pills. Once Beecher takes the first pill, he becomes addicted and must have his pills around 11 p.m. every night. At first people on the street report a prowler lurking behind trees, and Beecher wakes up with a worse headache and a grumpy disposition, even becoming surly with his daughter.

Three (or more) wonderful sequences occur, the first occurs in a bar/restaurant where Beecher confesses his addiction to his pills and asks his lovely nurse, Carol (Coleen Gray), to make sure she never gives him the pills, but when the doctor is called away, he finds a way to sneak the pills back into his possession. This sequence illustrates the tremendous acting performance that Beal creates in this quasi Mr. Hyde/junkie performance. We feel sympathetic toward Dr. Beecher because he was the victim of an accident, yet we see the monster that this formerly beloved town physician and single-parent is slowly becoming. For a B horror production, John Beal creates one memorable performance.

Later, Dr. Beaumont (the wonderful Dabbs Greer) and Beecher are alone working in Dr. Campbell's lab late at night. Beaumont, hoping that their scientific work will occupy his mind, takes Beecher's pills and locks them in a drawer. As the clock speeds closer and closer to 11 o'clock, Beecher becomes more unfocused and literally tries to claw inside the wooden desk drawer to get his pills. Beaumont's smile and reassuring voice only forces the good Beecher to bury his head in his hands, craving his medicine. However, in the best tradition of Jekyll and Hyde, Beecher turns into the vampire bat-fueled monster, without any need of the chemical, and in a spooky, shadowy sequence, attacks and kills his friend, who was only trying to cure him.

Perhaps the third memorable sequence involves misty scenes at night, as our silent vampire stalks the loveable old lady of the town. Her dog tries to fight off the fiend, but the poor lady goes down as the creepily just out-of-focus fiend goes for the jugular. In a similar sequence, the beautiful Coleen Gray is stalked in a similar fashion, but she is able to make it home before the monster can get her. These sequences are effectively spooky and easily raise audience goosebumps. The cinematography of Jack Mackenzie (who also filmed *The Return of Dracula*) excels in such sequences, and audiences literally screamed out loud during such scenes. The musical score of Gerald Fried also helps to maintain the chills and thrills.

Because the lead character, our tragic hero, is older than most B production heroes, as well as doomed to die, robust Kenneth Tobey plays the town sheriff, who ultimately saves Coleen Gray and destroys the vampire…with ordinary bullets noless! The climax and ending are slightly rushed, but what comes before is suburban Gothic at its best! Well-scripted and acted, *The Vampire* moves at a fast pace balancing these superb sequences of terror with building tension and suspense. For a B production, *The Vampire* becomes a textbook case in how to do it right. And John Beal portrays one of the most heart-wrenching mad doctors ever.

Gary J. Svehla

The Wasp Woman
Allied Artists/Filmgroup, 1959; Director: Roger Corman

The popular 1950s theme of rejuvenation and eternal youth was the subject of one of Roger Corman's final quickie black-and-white horror pictures, before he turned his attention to the works of Edgar Allan Poe. It's a swiftly moving horror-drama featuring a bravado performance from Susan Cabot, as the head of a cosmetics firm whose sales are falling at an alarming rate. When one of her salesman (Fred Eisley) has the audacity to suggest that the reason for the company's misfortunes lies in the fact that Cabot's looks, which advertise the firm's products, are not what they were 15 years earlier, when she was a stunner. The dowdy boss takes his comments under consideration, instead of firing him for his cheek. Enter Michael Mark as a professor, who claims to have created a rejuvenating serum from the enzymes present in the Royal Jelly of a queen wasp. Desperate for anything to put the company back on its feet, with the promise made by Mark of restoring her looks to their former beauty, Cabot hires the professor, who sets up his laboratory in her office block. Cabot undergoes a course of injections and, to her delight, her flawless skin returns and she looks years younger. However, impatience gets the better of her. She wants to look like a 20-something *now*, not in three months' time, so sneaking into Mark's lab at night, she injects herself and starts the ball rolling for a massive publicity campaign to promote the new age-preventing cosmetic. Then Mark disappears, knocked down in the street and rushed to the hospital in a coma, and Cabot takes one injection too many, changing into a killer wasp monster with carnivorous tendencies, killing one of her colleagues and a night watchman. Shot in darkened rooms, Cabot's wasp makeup, simply resembling a Halloween mask, isn't all that convincing because we can hardly see it. But the actress makes the most of what she has, pouncing on her victims to the sound of a droning wasp, and vampirizing them. The professor, back from the hospital, puts paid to the wasp creature in the climax by hurling a jar full of carbolic acid into her face, just as she is about to attack Eisley and Barboura Morris, who are snooping around, trying to discover the real secret behind the new cosmetic. Cabot is pushed backward through a window and falls to her death. Leo Gordon's tight script made the most of what by now was pretty much formulaic material, and all Corman's pictures were a cut above

Reel Mad Doctors

the average anyway, making *The Wasp Woman* a diverting little horror movie from the director's extensive stable.

Barry Atkinson

The Werewolf
Columbia, 1956; Director: Fred F. Sears

He was known as "Jungle Sam" in some circles for producing so many jungle adventures and serials, but the generally disparaged producer of Columbia's Bs, Sam Katzman, is due for re-evaluation. As a child the name Katzman, like Ed Wood, was synonymous with grade-Z productions, and it was fashionable to trash Katzman. But now seen in hindsight, his horror productions are iconic and quite entertaining. A generation or two ago, everyone laughed at the thought of Katzman as a horror film entrepreneur, but when his films are watched today, a new respect is dawning.

Sam Katzman's 1956 *The Werewolf* is a film woefully ignored for too long. This film is one of the true B gems of the 1950s, and under the direction of Fred F. Sears, becomes an emotionally involving experience. Most of the kudos for the success of the production must go to unknown star Steven Ritch, who plays the car accident victim is turned into a werewolf by two unscrupulous doctors, who feel the radiation released from nuclear explosions will soon change the entire human race into primitive animals. Ritch, playing husband and father Duncan Marsh, looses his memory and wanders into a northern California mountain/Western-style town (the entire movie was actually filmed on location), trying to understand who and what he is. Ritch's face always registers pain, confusion and terror. He is a family man, a salesman, who only wishes to return home; yet, he remembers enough of his werewolf escapades that he does not wish to endanger his family, so he hides out in the snow-covered woods. To create the modern day Western flavor, we have B Western star Harry Lauter playing the deputy to Don Megowan's sheriff (Megowan played the humanized, land-based Creature in *The Creature Walks Among Us*, and he played the Frankenstein Monster in Hammer's TV pilot, *Tales of Frankenstein*). These lawman are generally knuckleheaded boobs, who follow the letter of the law, claiming that sometimes they cannot save everyone. Sympathy comes from the elderly town doctor (Ken Christy) and his niece nurse (Joyce Holden), who plead sympathy and mercy for Marsh when the sheriff and his crew seem to only wish to hunt the man/beast down and kill him.

Wonderful horror sequences abound. In one scene the evil duo of scientists catch up to the cowering Marsh, who is hiding in a cave. However, when under pressure or stress, Marsh turns into the werewolf, which he does in marvelous time-lapse photography, finally drooling from his lower mouth as he pounces upon the doctor. The werewolf makeup is very similar to the Andreas makeup from Columbia's *Return of the Vampire,* over a decade earlier. Later, we have another wonderful scene when the werewolf, searching for food in the wild, carelessly steps into a trap and struggles to escape, limps away and gains audience sympathy. In fact, Marsh's original appearance in town first established such sympathy, when he is robbed as he leaves a bar late at night. As Marsh backs into a dark alley he is robbed by one of the patrons of his last $20, the two struggle as Marsh turns into the wolf, but this is unseen to the audience. The werewolf wins the struggle and exits from the alley. An old woman screams as the audience views the werewolf from the rear, but only in shadows. The film's dual climactic sequences are both gems. In the first, our two evil docs break into the jail to kidnap Marsh to continue experimenting on him, but little do they know that he is faking sleep…as the werewolf. In a wonderfully photographed sequence, the distorted shadows of the jail's bars are projected on the back wall as the werewolf flings the two humans across the cell—more as rag dolls than human beings. And of course, once the doctors are dead, Marsh escapes. This leads to the final pursuit of the werewolf, the sheriff and men carrying torches that they fling at the hapless wolf. The werewolf is cornered and crosses a stone ledge along the side of a bridge that overlooks the lake. The sheriff and his posse wait for Marsh. who is a sitting duck, and open fire, shooting him in the shoulder and gut. They kill the wolfman, who returns to his human form in death. Director Fred Sears works diligently to establish Marsh's sympathetic character, leaving the audience with mixed feelings at the sad death of the tragic victim turned crazed killer, who faces death to save his family.

The Werewolf shines because of its odd-for-the-time mountain location shooting (with Marsh running barefoot in the actual snow), its wonderful supporting cast of characters, its cleverly conceived werewolf encounters and mostly the terrific performance by Steven Ritch, who delivers one of the impressive horror performances of the decade.

Gary J. Svehla

Bride of Frankenstein
and
The Legacy of Dr. Pretorius

by William Max Miller

James Whale opens his 1935 masterpiece *Bride of Frankenstein* by pulling viewers out of the opulent luxury of a Regency drawing room and hurling them into the penumbral depths of the Dark Ages. After a short prologue showing Lord Byron and Percy Shelley discussing *Frankenstein* with Mary Shelley, in a luxuriant room the size of an airport hanger, the cultured poets and writers witness a sudden invasion from a less civilized world.

As we are told that the Monster survived the flames of the old mill where he had been trapped at the end of the previous film, the fiery skeleton of a building, burning luridly against a somber, troubled horizon, appears like a spectral painting on the wall of the parlor in which the elegant three sit. Small and distant at first, the portentous image grows until it encompasses the entire field of view with a sulfurous incandescence, and we can now make out an angry mob surging tumultuously around the burning edifice, starkly silhouetted by its flames. As the shrieks and cries of the mob grow louder, we become engulfed by the violent spectacle and realize that we have completely left the enlightened 19th century world of Byron and the Shelleys and entered a shadowy, indistinct dimension more in harmony with the Middle Ages. But it is not the chivalrous, romantic Middle Ages of Scott or Dumas to which James Whale transports us. Instead, he takes us to the demon-haunted landscapes of Hieronymus Bosch, where conflagrations seethe on the horizon and damnation waits in every shadow.

It is within this specially devised world of fuming smoke, hellfire and spiritual peril—so different from the austere naturalism of Frankenstein—that Whale introduces us to a figure completely new to the *Frankenstein* corpus: a macabre mad scientist named Dr. Pretorius, who coerces and connives a reluctant Henry Frankenstein back into the blasphemous

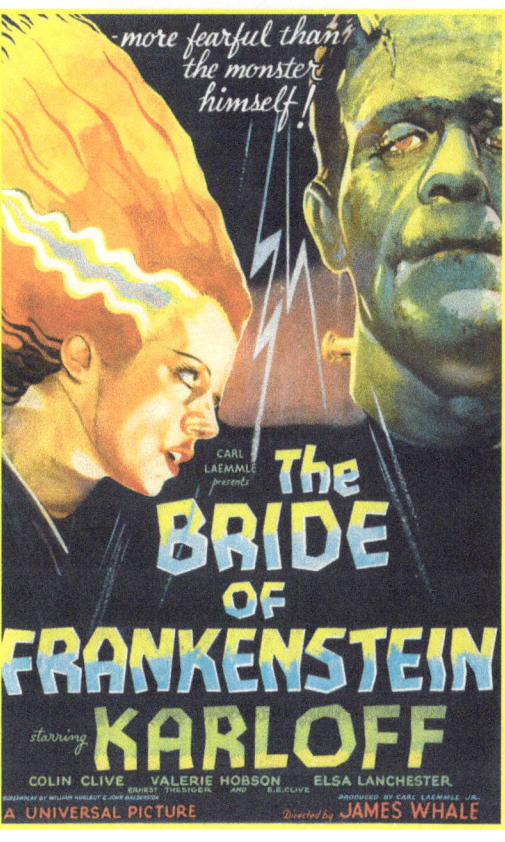

business of creating artificial life. The burning mill scene, so reminiscent of Bosch's nightmarish renderings of the apocalypse, provides the perfect point of entry into the dark universe of Pretorius, which, like a medieval painting of Heaven and Hell, is a world of gods and monsters. By blending the divine aspirations of alchemy with a very modern predilection for serial homicide and sadism, Pretorius navigates the Faustian and necrophilic undercurrents of the Frankenstein mythos more skillfully than any other character in subsequent films.

The role of Pretorius was assigned to the distinguished British actor Ernest Thesiger, a personal friend of director Whale's. Thesiger's ominous appearance and quirky delivery combine to create an aura of menace enlivened by gallows humor, which compliments perfectly the eccentric ambiance Whale created for the film. Described in 1935 by *Time* as the most "convincingly lunatic a scientist as ever reached the screen,"[1] Thesiger's portrayal of the demented alchemist is unforgettable. With it, Whale transforms *Bride of Frankenstein* into a kind of alchemical parable, a dark version of *The Chemical Wedding* in which Pretorius plays the role of an infernal matchmaker, who attempts to forge an unholy union of monsters. Far from playing only a colorful supporting role, he is crucial to the story, the very center around which the mythic whirlpool of *Bride of Frankenstein* revolves.

Tall, cadaverously thin, pale and parchment-faced, Pretorius dominates the movie. His wild eyes, tousled thatch of white hair and ruthless determination to realize his insane ambition all clearly mark him as a dangerous lunatic. Like an animated skeleton from a 14th-century Danse Macabre, Pretorius pirouettes between the laboratory and the crypt blithely, and seems equally comfortable in the company of both the living and the dead. An enthusiastic graveyard visitor, he cheerfully dines among coffins and corpses, always

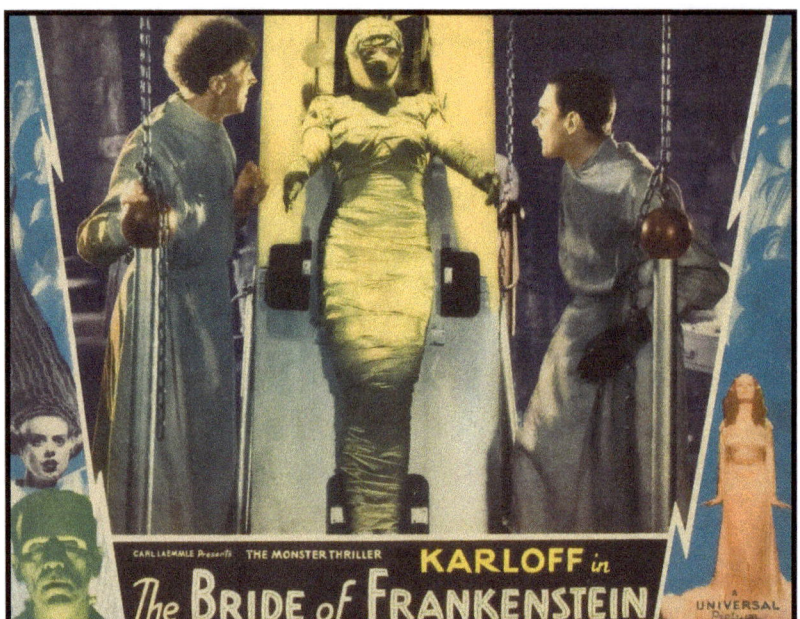

Dr. Pretorius (Ernest Thesiger), admires the Bride (Elsa Lanchester), as does Dr. Frankenstein (Colin Clive).

ready to entertain any monster that happens to drop by. Part scientist, part necromancer, Pretorius bridges the dark chasm which divides amoral modern science from the immoral Black Arts. He is also an early example of a type of monster that has become very prominent in the violent arena of our own contemporary cinema: the psychopathic serial killer who derives a sick thrill from murder and mutilation.

Pretorius functions as the demonic prime mover, who starts the infernal chain-reaction that finally explodes at the film's climax. Like Frankenstein, he has also created artificial life "in God's own image," but wearies of his tiny, doll-like creations and hatches a scheme to enlist the aid of Henry Frankenstein, his former pupil, in the fabrication of a female monster with whom Frankenstein's own oversized creation may breed. Stopping at nothing, Pretorius pillages graves, kidnaps and merrily murders his way through much of the film, in order to achieve this ghastly objective.

As is befitting for such a perilous character, Pretorius makes a very dramatic entrance onto the solemn stage of *Bride of Frankenstein*—an entrance which, when taken within the context of Whale's other works, immediately defines him as the film's major fiend. He first appears soon after Frankenstein has been carried home, presumably dead from the burning mill. After Frankenstein revives unexpectedly, he and his bride Elizabeth retire to their vast Gothic bedroom to contemplate the glorious folly of monster-making. After warning her husband that his insane dream of "creating living men from the dust of the dead" is "blasphemous," "wicked" and inspired by the devil himself, Elizabeth experiences a terrifying precognition of a death-like figure drawing near and reaching out for Henry.

At that precise moment, a resounding knock is heard at the castle door. Minnie, the eternally over-reactive maid, opens the gigantic portal cautiously and we get our first good look at Dr. Pretorius. It does not overly predispose us in his favor! Dressed in a funereal black cloak, dimly illumined by the pale light of Minnie's flickering candle, we see Pretorius' gaunt figure framed in the doorway, looming malevolently against the darkness of the stormy night. His intensely black, avian eyes glitter coldly from beneath the overshadowing brim of a large black hat, and his unnaturally arched, almost skull-like, nostrils flare like those of a predatory ghoul at the scent of blood.

Clearly, this is no ordinary visitor!

In Whale's films, closed and bolted doors convey a sense of security, and opening them gives the audience a thrill of intense vulnerability. In *Frankenstein*, the Monster's first appearance is through an opening door, backward at first, then followed by increasingly closer views of his scarred and sutured visage. Whale reuses this cinematic device in *The Invisible Man* when we catch our first startling glimpse of the bandaged and goggled features of Claude Rains, framed by the open door of the Lion's Head Inn. And here, in *Bride of Frankenstein*, he employs the same visual semantics for the entrance of Pretorius, defining him as the real monster of the film. He is identified with the danger all of us fear may be lurking on the other side of our own locked doors.

After Minnie apprehensively ushers the sinister scientist into Frankenstein's bedroom and preliminary introductions are concluded, Pretorius superciliously informs Elizabeth that his business with Frankenstein is private. When she departs, the mad old doctor goes to work on Frankenstein and proposes immediately that they collaborate on a new fiend-making project. Although initially refusing to help Pretorius meddle any further in things best left alone, Frankenstein's curiosity quickly overcomes his scruples when the older man confides that he, too, has succeeded in creating artificial life. Frankenstein eagerly accompanies Pretorius back to his Caligari-like abode for a peek at the elderly savant's creations.

When commenting on Dr. Pretorius, recent writers claim to find covert sexual implications in this scene of the macabre doctor's midnight intrusion into Frankenstein's bedroom. They point to Pretorius' fussy mannerisms, his desire to get Frankenstein's wife out of the way and his attempts to persuade Frankenstein to become his partner in the creation of other living beings, and discern a subliminal homoerotic agenda concealed beneath these actions. David J. Skal, in his book *The Monster Show*, provides a good example of this sort of interpretation when he describes Thesiger's portrayal of Pretorius as an "over-the-top caricature of a bitchy and aging homosexual." He views Pretorius as a "gay Mephistopheles" who seduces Frankenstein away from the bridal bed with the promise of an improved method of procreation.[2]

Dr. Pretorius extends his arm to prevent the Monster (Boris Karloff) from approaching his "bride."

Although currently fashionable, such assessments project too many contemporary concerns onto a scene that seems designed to amplify the medieval, Bosch–like atmosphere created in the opening sequence. By placing the forbidding Dr. Pretorius at Frankenstein's bedside, Whale alludes to another well-known image from Medieval art, which first came into vogue in Europe immediately following the ravages of the Black Plague. At that time, disturbing depictions of skeletal Grim Reapers and their graphically decomposing victims reminded traumatized plague survivors of the ultimate uncertainty of life,[3] and went on to metamorphose into the iconic images of later horror literature and film.[4] One particular vignette frequently employed by the artists of this grim period shows an unfortunate person reclining in the false security of his bed while a frightening figure of Death, in all his emaciated glory, silently creeps up to the bedside.[5] That Whale intended his scene of Pretorius in the bedroom to evoke echoes of this somber artistic tradition is made apparent by the film's dialogue: "It comes! A figure like death!" the hysterical Elizabeth announces, as Pretorius begins pounding at the castle door. As the film unwinds, her terrifying intuition about the deathly Dr. Pretorius proves to be well-founded.

Even if we ignore Whale's allusion to the Dance of Death motif, we still can not accept Skal's evaluation of Pretorius, because it's almost impossible to conceive of the withered old scientist as engaging in any sort of intimate sexual relationship, be it gay or straight. The man seems too cold and brittle to have such desires. At most, as the famous scene of his macabre little banquet in the crypt should make obvious, Pretorius had necrophilic tendencies. It is possible to see him deriving a ghoulish, intellectualized pleasure while dissecting dead human tissues, but also very difficult to imagine him jumping anyone's bones—unless, of course, all the flesh has been removed from them!

That Whale conceived Pretorius as a homicidal necrophile would have been more obvious had the squeamish censors of the mid-1930s not excised a significant scene in which Pretorius explains to Frankenstein the reason why he had been "booted out" of the university, where Frankenstein had once been instructed by him. As reported by Forrest J Ackerman, who saw an uncensored studio preview of *Bride*, Pretorius admitted to Frankenstein that he had been forced to resign due to a horrible incident in the dissection room. After obtaining the body of a woman known to suffer from cataleptic seizures, Pretorius "mistakes" her for dead and begins carving into her. When she finally revives and screams, Pretorius does "the only merciful thing" and puts her out of her misery. While maintaining his innocence, Pretorius nevertheless lets slip that he did think the body felt suspiciously warm when he began dissecting![6]

This gruesome little episode, considered too shocking for audiences of the 1930s, sounds dismally routine to followers of contemporary newscasts, who are quite familiar with the serial killer's penchant for mutilating and molesting his victims. We have grown calloused to the psychosexual atrocities of monsters like Pretorius. But in 1935, Whale was forced to conceal such deviant acts behind veiled allusions and double entendres. Earlier in the film, Pretorius explained to Elizabeth that he had been kicked out of the university

The Monster and Dr. Pretorius team up to bully Dr. Frankenstein into creating a woman.

"for knowing too much." The superficial implication is that Pretorius likes to think his ex-colleagues resented his superior intellect, but when taken within the context of the censored dissection room episode, one suspects that the "knowing" for which Pretorius got sacked should be interpreted in a Biblical and necrophilic sense!

But it is with a single memorable close-up of the mad doctor's wrinkled face that Whale best reveals Pretorius' true sexual inclinations. Back at his own laboratory, Pretorius explains to Frankenstein his plans of making a female monster. When it dawns on Frankenstein just what Pretorius wants him to help create, he stammers in disbelief: "You mean...?" and leaves the startling thought unfinished. "Yes. A woman!" Pretorius concludes, as the camera closes in on his demonic features. "That should be really interesting!" His eyes gleam with lascivious anticipation and his lips curl into a lewd sneer.

It is hard to understand how Skal (or anyone else) could view this scene and still imagine that Pretorius was gay. This is the closest Pretorius ever comes in the entire film to betraying any sign of sexual interest, and that interest is so lecherously heterosexual and necrophilic that it approaches the archetypal. You can almost see the scalpels coldly glitter in the cadaverous old scientist's wild eyes, and understand that visions of dead, vulnerable female flesh are performing a morbid striptease in his mind. Yet Skal manages to miss this completely.

In all fairness to Skal, Pretorius did act prissy and effete at certain points in the movie, but only when it was to his advantage to appear that way. Like Ted Bundy, he was essentially a lethal con-man who wanted to manipulate others, and his sociopathic enterprises were greatly facilitated by behaving in ways that would cause people to underestimate his true threat potential. In his initial dealings with Frankenstein, Pretorius does indeed come across as a bit of an eccentric sissy, whom one would never suspect would even be able to handle the sight of blood. But when interacting with his henchmen, Karl and Ludwig, the true Pretorius comes out.

In the movie's famous crypt sequence, we see Pretorius and his grave-robbing cronies entering a vast, moldy catacomb. Karl and Ludwig, self-proclaimed murderers, are almost overcome with fear, but Pretorius advances bravely into the shadows, barking out orders like a hardened crime boss. Here, Pretorius is no sissy. We see him as he really is: cold, dominant and utterly ruthless. This is the side of his personality that Pretorius wishes to conceal from Frankenstein, whose cooperation he needs.

Pretorius immediately enters a fenced-in area of the crypt where several dust-covered coffins rest in funereal gloom. After only a cursory inspection, he indicates the coffin that his lackeys are to rifle. Pretorius' quick confidence concerning his selection of coffins hints at a significant familiarity with these melancholy precincts of the dead, acquired through regular and frequent visits, and thickens the miasma of necrophilia which surrounds him. He knows what he wants because he has browsed here before.

After he threatens to send Karl and Ludwig to the gallows if they won't cooperate, the two fugitives reluctantly pry open the lid of the coffin. We catch but a tantalizing glimpse of the cobwebbed skeleton reposing within. "Pretty little thing, in her way," Karl comments, while ogling the female's remains, but Pretorius has other intentions and seems undaunted by such aesthetic considerations. "I hope her bones are firm!" he states, the unconcealed excitement in his voice making him sound like a philanderer eagerly scrutinizing a prostitute he has just picked up.

After paying Karl and Ludwig and telling them they may go, Pretorius explains that he plans on staying for a while. "I rather like this place!" he cheerfully exclaims, further revealing his abnormal tastes. Once alone, Pretorius settles down for a pleasant interlude among the moldering bones of the dead, and the film's crowning moment of the macabre unfolds.

In an obvious parody of a romantic dinner-for-two, Pretorius lights candles, uncorks a bottle of fine wine and sets out a roast chicken on the lid of the coffin he has just rifled. His lady companion of the evening grins fleshlessly at him from the center of the coffin lid, where he has meticulously arranged her stolen bones into the kind of decorative centerpiece. Pretorius enjoys satisfying his appetites thoroughly here in the

crypt, and his hearty laughter echoes incongruously in a place usually reserved for sorrow and weeping.

To view this withered ghoul as being "wildly effeminate," as a recent commentator in *Films in Review* does,[7] is to border on the misogynistic. Thanks to modern police profiling techniques, it is easy to recognize patterns in Pretorius' behaviors in the crypt, which duplicate some of the ritualistic actions engaged in by serial killers. His practice of eating in intimate proximity to decomposing corpses and his decorative use of human bones are regular features of ritualized homicide. Whale's perceptive use of such details was probably intuitive: The revolting actions of a necrophile like Ed Gein, who accented the interior of his home with trophies fashioned from his victims' body parts and used human skulls for soup bowls, would not make tabloid headlines for another 22 years.[8] But Whale may have been influenced by Fritz Lang's 1931 movie *M*, in which Peter Lorre portrayed a character based on serial killer Peter Kurten, better known as the Dusseldorf Ripper.[9] While far less cerebral and organized than Pretorius, Kurten also practiced the arts of human vivisection and necrophilia in his own crude fashion, and Whale may have sharpened Pretorius' scalpel on Lang's German model.

As Pretorius savors his sepulchral picnic, we see Frankenstein's Monster creep from the shadows toward the cackling mad scientist. Hearing sounds behind him, Pretorius turns and confronts the seven-foot fiend who has been terrorizing the countryside. His reaction at this point is remarkable: Without even so much as a single sign of being startled, Pretorius rapidly assesses his unusual situation and calmly speaks to the Monster. "Oh," he says, "I thought I was alone!" And without further pause he bids the Monster to share his meal, all the while informing the creature enthusiastically that the skeletal remains, which grace their makeshift table, are for use in the body of its future female mate.

These are hardly the reactions of a character from *La Cage aux Folles*! No other person in *Bride of Frankenstein*, except the blind hermit, was able to penetrate beyond the horrifying external appearance of the Monster and react to it with anything but terror. But whereas the blind hermit "saw" the creature's innate goodness, Pretorius recognized immediately its potential for evil, and began to scheme how he could use this dark force to persuade Frankenstein to collaborate with him. This scene is clearly designed to contrast Pretorius with the hermit, and places him in the same spiritual perspective by defining him as the Satanic counterweight to the hermit's Christ-like compassion.

As Dr. Pretorius explains his dream of creating a synthetic female, the Monster lifts the skull from its place on the coffin lid and, staring wistfully into its empty eye-sockets, intones the lines which Stephen King finds so chilling:[10] "I...

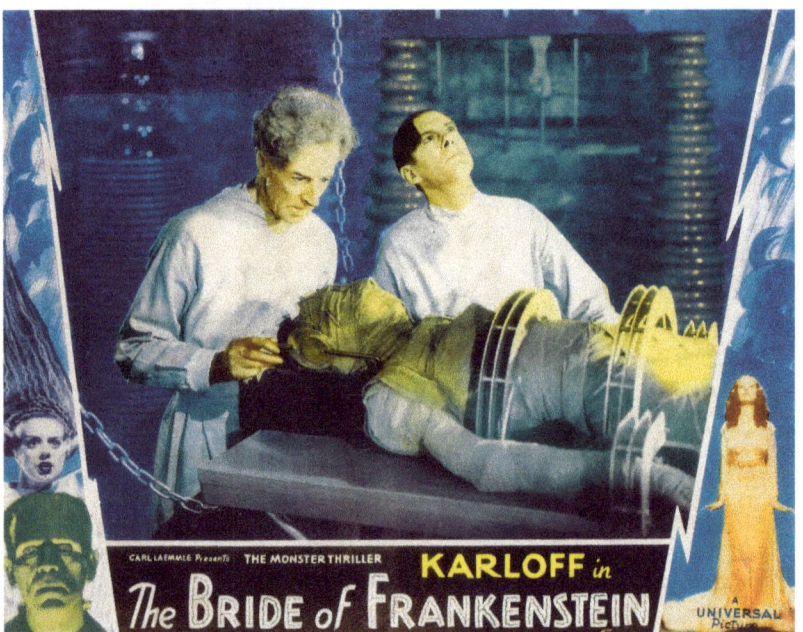

As Dr. Frankenstein looks skyward, Dr. Pretorius looks into the face of the corpse, ready to be reborn as the bride.

love...dead," his clumsy lips struggle with the words, "hate living." This awkward recitation of the Necrophile's Creed immediately elicits Pretorius' approval. "You are wise in your generation!" he compliments the Monster, again disclosing the appalling nature of his own depraved preferences. There is nothing gay about this morbid man at all, and even the most rabid homophobe would approve of open homosexuality before condoning the kind of ghoulish perversions in which Pretorius seems to indulge.

Pretorius' mortuary soiree with the Monster, with its distinctively necrophilic overtones, reveals him to be a prominent citizen of the world of monsters. But there is much more to Pretorius than simple ghastliness and perversity. In the scene where he takes Frankenstein back to his "humble abode" and shows him his own miniature creations, we enter the world of a man who would be God.

Pretorius ushers Frankenstein into a dwelling of oppressive shadows and disorienting angles in which only he and Dr. Caligari could ever possibly feel at home. They enter a room filled with dark Victorian furniture, crumbling leather volumes, bubbling chemical apparatus and an overwhelming sense of menace, greatly enhanced by the presence of a skeleton suspended in one corner. Two death masks hang on the walls in the distance, above the good doctor's bed, and something that resembles a flayed human hand dangles grotesquely from the rafters.

After offering Frankenstein a glass of gin, Pretorius proposes an appropriate toast for the occasion: "To a new world, of gods and monsters!" He downs his glass (a laboratory beaker) with a sinister chuckle, then retires into a back room, while Frankenstein waits impatiently. Pretorius returns carrying a large, coffin-shaped box, his face contorted into a frowning grimace by its weight. The camera moves in as he opens the box and reveals the startling results of his arcane experiments. Instead of something monstrous and frightening, as the viewer has been led to expect, Pretorius shows off a charming set of miniature humanoids, alive and well, each one housed in its own private bottle!

This episode strikes most viewers as something straight out of *Gulliver's Travels* or *Alice in Wonderland*. In a recent issue of *Filmfax*, Bryan Senn (who may have been quoting Boris Karloff—his punctuation makes this unclear) refers to this scene as the "regrettable homunculi sequence" which "detracts from the film."[11] Some viewers dislike this interlude involving the little bottled people because they apparently miss the subtle visual metaphor that Whale works into the episode. During a series of close-ups showing the diminutive creatures (which significantly include a king, a queen and a bishop), the camera occasionally moves back for long shots of Pretorius looming above his tiny synthetic beings, like a gigantic chess player craftily moving his pieces on the sinister board, over which he and Frankenstein face off. Whale's symbolism is clear: In choosing to accompany Pretorius back to his home, Frankenstein has unwittingly entered the game that the older scientist is playing. Pretorius is slyly maneuvering Frankenstein into position for some dreadful checkmate, which will finally coerce his total cooperation. He is the arch manipulator who uses people like chess pieces to further his own evil ends.

The homunculi sequence further defines the deranged physician's character by having him identify himself with one of the tiny creatures. "Very bizarre, this little chap," Pretorius says as he shows Frankenstein a bottled simulacrum of the devil, complete with pointed beard and cape. "There's a certain resemblance to me, don't you think?" There certainly is! As the film unwinds, Pretorius is revealed as a Mephistophelean influence who drags the Faustian Frankenstein ever downward into perdition.[12]

"Why, this isn't science!" gasps Frankenstein after viewing Pretorius' living chessmen. "It's more like black magic!" His evaluation of the homunculi is penetrating, for these miniature beings forge strong links between Pretorius and the shadowy world of alchemy, black magic and the occult in several important ways. They are strangely reminiscent of the haunting, supernatural fantasies of E.T.A. Hoffmann, one of which (*The Golden Pot*) contains an episode about tiny men trapped in bottles on a shelf. Pretorius' bottled creatures also evoke images from the Tarot deck, in which symbolic representations of kings, queens, bishops and the devil figure prominently. (The Tarot pack also contains a Hanged Man swinging on a scaffold, a Hermit, a Grim Reaper, a mob wielding clubs and a Tower Struck by God—all images which appear in Whale's two *Frankenstein* films. It would be interesting to find out if Whale was familiar with Tarot symbolism.)

The fact that Pretorius grew his creatures chemically also associates him with yet another sinister, arcane personage: Paracelsus, the 16th-century alchemist and occultist, who was also credited with the creation of homunculi via the curious method of placing his semen in airtight jars buried in horse manure for 40 days, and then nurturing the resultant creatures with human blood![13] Whale hints that Pretorius employed an equally seminal technique in the creation of his own Lilliputian brood, when he has Pretorius explain to Frankenstein that he "grew" his creatures "as Nature does, from seed." In her novel, Mary Shelley relates that Frankenstein had first become interested in "natural philosophy" (i.e., chemistry) through reading the works of alchemists, among them Paracelsus.[14] Whale was being faithful to Shelley's prototype when he portrayed his Frankenstein as a former student of the homunculi-creating Pretorius.

The tower laboratory of Pretorius and Frankenstein, with assistant Karl (Dwight Frye) working for Pretorius to acquire fresh human organs.

Critics who dislike the homunculi sequence in *Bride of Frankenstein* seem unaware of its many metaphorical and symbolic nuances. Far from being Whale's self-indulgent excursion into whimsy, it is one of the pivotal scenes of the film, defining the character and role of Pretorius and unmistakably helping to identify him with dark, infernal forces. It operates just like a page from a medieval alchemical manuscript, which conceals its real meaning behind a misleading facade of absurdity.

The deeper Luciferian motivations of Pretorius would be much easier for contemporary interpreters to discern if they could move beyond the popular notion that the enterprise in which he and Frankenstein engage is essentially reproductive, a kind of male method of making babies without the participation of women. Feminist writers like Anne K. Mellor argue that men of the monster-making persuasion want to avoid intercourse and the female womb altogether, so that they can usurp the female's ability to have children.[15] James B. Twitchell champions this kind of interpretation when, in his book *Dreadful Pleasures*, he comments that Colin Clive's exuberant lines at the climactic moment of his monster's creation in Frankenstein should be "In the name of God! Now I know what it's like to be mother!"[16]

It has become trendy to interpret the Frankenstein myth in such a fashion and it is this perspective that props up the interpretation of Pretorius as a homosexual seducer. But in spite of its popularity, this view trivializes the real intent behind the insane project of creating artificial life. It assumes that a crazed laboratory creator like Pretorius wants to bypass sex with a woman, while still managing to create another human being. But it really isn't sex and the female womb that such a lunatic scientist is so obsessively trying to circumvent. What he's actually trying to avoid is the creation of a human being.

An important clue lies in the fact that Pretorius and Frankenstein do not merely wish to reanimate the dead. If that were their goal, why not simply exhume and experiment upon a single body? Why dig up, dissect and reconnect all those different body parts? But the reanimation of a dead individual would merely bring about the return to life of a human individual, a person with parents of his own and an established heritage over which his reanimators could not claim creative authorship. In short, such a revitalized dead person would perhaps owe his reanimators an immense debt of gratitude for returning him to the land of the living. But supremely ambitious men like Pretorius and Frankenstein want their creatures to owe them more than simple gratitude. Much more.

By using parts from many different bodies, Pretorius and Frankenstein could obliterate (or hope to obliterate) all recognizable traces of an independent human lineage, for only by so doing would they feel absolutely responsible for their Monsters' creation. In turn, the Monsters would owe their entire existence to the creative will of Pretorius and Frankenstein alone and would have the same relationship to them that humans have to God. "A new species would bless me as its creator and source,"[17] Frankenstein plainly states his intentions in Shelley's novel. "No father could claim the gratitude of his child as completely as I should..."[18] Obviously, the reanimated corpse of a single individual could never satisfy such grandiose demands. And so the creatures of Pretorius and Frankenstein had to be non-humanly conceived out of organic flotsam and jetsam, which no longer retained any identifiable connection with a particular human genealogy.

"Let us create a race, a manmade race upon the face of the Earth," urges Pretorius. This is the true essence of the "mad dream" to which Pretorius recalls Frankenstein. He is a man who wants to play the role of God to a race of artificial beings of his own creation. The enterprise in which Pretorius enlists Frankenstein's aid is essentially Promethean because it usurps the prerogative of vital creation from God and presumptuously places it in the unworthy hands of mere mortals. The arrogant toast proposed by Pretorius, with its flamboyant reference to gods and monsters, succinctly states the case. We know who the monsters are. The gods will be their makers.

There is no homosexuality here, no desire to become a woman or play the female role in the creative act. The female role alone, since it is still just a human role, would also be much too limited to fulfill such an egomaniacal desire for apotheosis. Instead, Pretorius and Frankenstein share the same kind of power fantasy that overwhelmed so many other doctors in Europe at the time *Bride of Frankenstein* was made. This fantasy was achieving a hideous reality in 1935, not in some Gothic tower laboratory, but in the developing prison camps of the Nazis where real life imitations of Dr. Pretorius employed selective sterilization and genocide rather than lightning bolts in their murderous bid to create a manmade master race.

Trendy, contemporary interpretations of Dr. Pretorius, which fabricate homosexual or mysogynistic motivations, fall short of the mark. Pretorius does not envy women, and is not trying to supplant them by usurping their reproductive role, for to do so would still fail to achieve his inflated objectives. The scientific partnership between Pretorius and Frankenstein is not a kind of intellectualized or sublimated homosexuality, because it has to be completely asexual in order to succeed. Sexuality of any sort—straight or gay—has to be totally transcended because sexuality is a human activity and Pretorius aspires to be divine. Mere reproduction is not his aim. The more ambitious goal of original production is what he hopes to accomplish, for only this will satisfy his Satanic ambition to make himself the equal of God.

The movies themselves make it unmistakably obvious that it is God and not heterosexuality that is being defied. In the prologue to *Frankenstein*, Edward Van Sloan warns us that the shocking tale we are to see concerns a man who chose to act "without reckoning upon God." The opening of *Bride of Frankenstein* provides a more specific and detailed explanation: "My purpose was to write a moral lesson," Whale has Mary Shelley herself explain, "of the punishment that befell a mortal man who dared to emulate God." It is sad that so many contemporary writers completely ignore such straightforward statements.[19]

Myopic perspectives, which view Pretorius as a homosexual caricature and reduce *Bride of Frankenstein* to the shrunken status of a "cartoony sex parable,"[20] are analogous to viewing a painting like Hieronymus Bosch's *Garden of Earthly Delights* (with its cavorting naked throngs) as being a medieval European version of an Oriental sex manual, like the *Kama Sutra*!

Of all the innumerable *Frankenstein* adaptations, this film stands out because of its unparalleled exploration of the religious themes inherent to the subject matter. This exploration is greatly facilitated by the presence of Dr. Pretorius, who thoroughly and masterfully elucidates the spiritual and monstrous turbulence of the Frankenstein myth. With his more-than-mortal ambition, and his depraved sexual ghoulishness, Pretorius remains one of the most memorable representatives of the world of gods and monsters that American film has yet produced.

1. *Time* Magazine. Quoted in *Famous Monsters of Filmland* #21 (Feb. 1963) p. 74.
2. David J. Skal, *The Monster Show*. Penguin Books, 1993. pp. 185, 187.
3. Philip Ziegler, *The Black Death*. Harper Torchbooks, 1971. p. 275.
4. Walter Kendrick, in *The Thrill of Fear* (Grove Press, 1991) thoroughly traces this evolution.
5. Walter Bosing, *Hieronymus Bosch*. Taschen, 1987. p. 32.
6. Forrest J Ackerman, *Famous Monsters of Filmland* #21 (Feb. 1963) pp. 44-46.
7. *Films in Review*. Quoted by Frank J. Dello Stritto in *Cult Movies* #21, p. 32.
8. Paul Anthony Woods, *Ed Gein—Psycho*. St. Martin's Press, 1995.
9. Moira Martingale, *Cannibal Killers*. St. Martin's Press, 1995. pp. 35-40.
10. Stephen King, *Danse Macabre*. Berkeley Books, 1983. p. 52.
11. Bryan Senn, *Filmfax* #58 (Oct. 1996-Jan. 1997) p. 70.
12. Paul M. Jensen, in *The Men Who Made the Monsters* (Twayne Publishers, 1996) p. 45, describes an edited scene, which further strengthened Pretorius' identification with Lucifer. After seeing Pretorius with his tiny bottled creations, Karl declares to Ludwig, "He is the Devil, I tell you!"
13. *Secrets of the Alchemists*, Time-Life Books, p. 69.
14. Mary W. Shelley, *Frankenstein*. Grosset and Dunlap, 1931 edition. pp. 29-30, 40.
15. Anne K. Mellor, *Mary Shelley, Her Life, Her Fiction, Her Monsters*. Routledge, 1989.
16. James B. Twitchell, *Dreadful Pleasures*. Oxford University Press, 1985. p. 182.
17. Mary W. Shelley, op. cit. p. 46.
18. Mary W. Shelley, ibid.
19. S.S. Prawer, in *Caligari's Children* (Da Capa Pess, Inc. 1980) p. 27, comments that the films make equally obvious visual statements of intent. At the beginning of the first film, while helping Fritz exhume a corpse, Frankenstein tosses a shovelful of dirt directly in the face of a statue of the Grim Reaper, which looms behind them in the graveyard. This defiant gesture toward death is repeated in *Bride of Frankenstein* when Pretorius blows smoke in the face of the skull during the crypt sequence. "Perhaps death is sacred, and I've profaned it," wonders a remorseful Frankenstein at the beginning of *Bride*. Death is portrayed as a divine limit placed on human endeavors, which Frankenstein and Pretorius defy. Clearly, these men are challenging something far more metaphysically daunting than sex role stereotypes!
20. David J. Skal, op. cit. p. 184.

Our Favorite Mad Doctors

1. Boris Karloff as Dr. Niemann in *House of Frankenstein*: "Now friend Daniel, Frankenstein would have severed the spinal cord here...but I'm not quite sure he was correct." Karloff was also great in *Frankenstein 1970*.
2. Bela Lugosi as Dr. Vornoff in *Bride of the Monster*: "Here in this forsaken jungle hell, Professor Strowsky, I have proved that I am all right!"
3. John Carradine as Dr. von Altermann in *Revenge of the Zombies*: "Ah—Hooooooo!"
4. Lionel Atwill as Dr. Ralph Benson in *The Mad Doctor of Market Street*: Atwill played mad docs in more movies than I can remember.
5. And finally... Horst Frank as Dr. Ood in *The Head*! Possibly the maddest doctor of them all!

All the above have provided inspiration and role models for us down through the years.
—Rockin' Lon Talbot

1. Bela Lugosi
2. Lionel Atwill
3. George Zucco
4. Peter Lorre (*Mad Love*)
5. Boris Karloff
(And if I could add one more?)
6. Colin Clive
—Arthur Lennig

1. Bela Lugosi
2. Lionel Atwill
3. Boris Karloff
4. John Carradine
5. George Zucco
—Dr. Vollin, MD

My top five favorite mad scientist flicks? Man, that's a toughie; so many to choose from! Here goes…
1. *The Devil Bat*—Who else but Bela Lugosi could turn an otherwise silly Poverty Row, no-budget PRC thriller into such an entertaining romp? Peppered with some classic mad scientist dialogue, *The Devil Bat* is raised from obscurity by Lugosi's over-the-top portrayal of Dr. Carruthers, an exploited scientist. Cheated and hung out to dry by a profiteering cosmetics firm (shades of Enron), Dr. Carruthers takes what he perceives to be justified revenge by turning his oppressors into walking guinea pigs with his giant bat-attracting aftershave. And nobody—nobody—could make a simple good-bye sound like such a death sentence!
2. *Frankenstein's Daughter*—This low-rent, cheesy movie features great portrayals. Mr. Frank's explanation of his elderly colleague's seemingly incredible behavior to the police is hilarious: "He's a little, well, you know."
3. *Die, Monster, Die*—Well past his prime in physical years (heck, he was already middle-aged when he got his vehicle role in *Frankenstein*), Boris Karloff is nevertheless at his prime in this movie. In the bedroom scene with his wife, Karloff's character sends chills of delight through the viewer's spine as he raises an eyebrow and says: "If there was evil, it was buried with him."
4. *Flesh for Frankenstein* (aka *Andy Warhol's Frankenstein*)—This is possibly Udo Kier's greatest career role. Chock-full of sexual weirdness, *Flesh For Frankenstein* is also a 3-D gore-fest. But never mind all that. Kier absolutely rocks!
5. *Bride of the Monster*—Long forgotten by the big shots at Universal and the other major Hollywood producers, Bela Lugosi delivers one of his swan song performances in Ed Wood's finest film. One final comeback attempt. One final good-bye. "Home...I have no home. Hunted. Despised. Living like an animal. The jungle is my home. But I will show the world that I can be its master. I will perfect my own race of people: a race of atomic supermen which will conquer the world!" Over the top. Played to the hilt. Pure Lugosi!
—Douglas Brown

Ultimate Mad Doctor Films:
1. *Metropolis* (1927): The ultimate evil scientist and his mad dream survive.
2. *Bride of Frankenstein* (1935): Why have one mad doctor when you can have two, each responsible for his own monster!

4. Bela Lugosi: *Murders in the Rue Morgue, The Raven, Dark Eyes of London, The Devil Bat.* Lugosi was absolutely splendid and uniquely different in each of these four films. Lugosi was actually a terrifically underrated mad doctor.
5. George Zucco: *The Mad Ghoul, Dr. Renault's Secret.* Zucco was extremely disturbing in *The Mad Ghoul*, lending that film its true moments of horror. He was also excellent in the supremely underrated *Dr. Renault's Secret*.
—Kenny Strong

1. Peter Cushing as Baron Frankenstein: Over the course of six films, Cushing so memorably defined Mary Shelley's Faustian protagonist that it is almost impossible to accept anyone else in the role. By turns heroic and evil, Cushing's Frankenstein is a fascinating study in the evolution of a role over the course of many years and movies. The conclusion of *Frankenstein and the Monster from Hell*, in which the character is revealed to be wholly insane, is shocking and even a little pathetic. Cushing is great in all of these films, but if I had to pick just one, I would have to go for his most sympathetic turn, in the criminally underappreciated *Evil of Frankenstein* (1964).
2. Vincent Price as Dr. Anton Phibes in *The Abominable Dr. Phibes* (1971): Billed as Price's 100th film (it wasn't), *The Abominable Dr. Phibes* gave the noted horror star a new kind of part to play in the autumn of his career—the wronged maniac who avenges himself on his foes in bizarrely comic ways. Dr. Phibes is neither a medico nor a scientist—he's an academic, with dual doctorates in music and theology. This is an interesting variation on the stereotype, and Price mines the film for every laugh. My favorite of his bits takes place after Phibes drains Dr. Longstreet (Terry-Thomas) of his blood: Phibes lingers to cast a disparaging eye towards one of Longstreet's paintings, in a great reference to Price's well-known expertise in art.
3. Jeffrey Combs as Herbert West in *Re-Animator* (1986): "You'll never get credit for my discoveries. Who'd believe a talking head? Get a job in a sideshow!" With that line, Jeffrey Combs immediately made my list of the cinema's maddest scientists. *Re-Animator* is a lot bloodier—and funnier—than the original Lovecraft serial that inspired the movie. It's also more entertaining than the group of stories ol' HPL himself ranked near the bottom of his output, and much of that fun factor is due to Combs' over-the-top performance as Herbert West.
4. Anthony Hopkins as Dr. Hannibal Lecter in *The Silence of the Lambs* (1991): It is probably an overdone choice, but what can I say? Hopkins won a well-deserved Oscar for his terrifying turn as the cannibalistic shrink; it's a performance that still works after more than a decade of sequels, rip-offs and parodies. The erudite and charming Dr. Lecter perfectly embodies the charm of evil that Terence Fisher used to go on about.
5. Fredric March as Dr. Henry Jekyll in *Dr. Jekyll and Mr. Hyde* (1932): The first time an actor won an Oscar for a horror part was also for portraying a mad doctor. True, March's Jekyll

3. *House of Dracula* (1945): The last classic Universal mad doctor (Onslow Stevens) is one of the best.
4. *Back to the Future* (1985): An homage to *Metropolis,* with Christopher Lloyd's Dr. Brown?
5. *Young Frankenstein* (1974): Gene Wilder creates an unforgettable homage.
—Scott Essman

1. Lionel Atwill: *Man Made Monster, The Vampire Bat* and *Ghost of Frankenstein.* No one had such malevolence in the 1930s and '40s as a mad doctor as Lionel Atwill. The only tragedy is he never had a definitive movie to play a mad doctor, but even just one of these is enough to get him on the top-five list, where he reigns as number one.
2. Colin Clive: Ultimately his Dr. Frankenstein is not as mad as Atwill's mad doctor, but just as devoted and maybe even more intense. Clive was the perfect man for the role in the Universal classics.
3. Boris Karloff: *The Man Who Changed His Mind* and many, many Columbia horror films. After 1935 Karloff seemed to play nothing but mad scientists. He was good in nearly all of them, and merits a place on this list.

isn't quite insane, but his alter ego, the brutish Mr. Hyde, certainly is. Even after more than 70 years, March's acting still packs a punch. Furthermore, the film itself is scarier than almost any other shocker from the Golden Age.
—Jonathan M. Lampley

In response to your request, here are my top-five favorite mad doctors:
1. Dr. Eric Vornoff: Bela's last speaking role, in Ed Wood's miserable *Bride of the Monster,* has always been one of my faves. Despite the threadbare surroundings, Lugosi gives one of his most enjoyable performances. And any doctor who thinks a photo enlarger will make one of his patients "as big as a giant, with the strength of 20 men" has to be mad!
2. Herbert West: Jeffrey Combs in *Re-Animator* delivers the first of many quirky performances that secured his position as one of the few (if only) current actors primarily identified with genre films. The movie is a memorably wild ride, and one of the best horror films of the 1980s.
3. Dr. Pretorius: My all-time favorite horror film features one of the all-time best mad doctors. A practitioner of black magic, one wonders what else might have transpired in his "humble abode." I wish Ernest Thesiger had made a few more appearances in horror films of the 1930s (other than *The Ghoul* or *They Drive By Night*, 1938). Might he have topped his most macabre performance?
4. Professor Dexter: Bela Lugosi in *Return of the Ape Man* delivers one of the juiciest mad doctor lines of all time: "Some people's brains would never be missed." This mad doctor is worthy of consideration for that profound observation alone!
5. Dr. Moreau: Charles Laughton's performance in *Island of Lost Souls* reeks of sadism and debauchery and stands out as one of the weirdest characterizations in all 1930s horror films (pre-Code or otherwise). He was definitely mad, and that's why he makes my list!
—Tom Shumaker

1. I just have to mention a favorite mad doctor scene. In *Doctor X,* with Lionel Atwill and Fay Wray, there is a scene with Preston Foster in which he transforms into the midnight killer, while chanting "synthetic flesh, synthetic flesh!" That must be one of the best mad lab scenes ever.
   Okay, four more...
2. Peter Lorre in *Mad Love*. He is just so eye-bugging mad.
3. Colin Clive, for both his performances as Dr. Frankenstein. He is so wired. He would be a great mad doctor even if he did not happen to be re-animating dead tissue.
4. Rotwang from *Metropolis*...I had to mention at least one German expressionist mad doctor.
5. I almost forgot to mention Ernest Thesiger as Dr. Pretorius... "Gin, it's my only weakness." This is my top six list.
6. Last but not least: Dr. Jekyll in the 1932 version of *Dr. Jekyll and Mr. Hyde,* with Fredric March. That film had the classic combination of great mad lab scenes and a scientist who is a genius (but still thinks it might be smart to use himself as

a test subject). March is my favorite Mr. Hyde because he gives Hyde an animal quality. Sort of ape-like, cat-like, I don't know. But I believe him as Hyde.
—J. Lansberg

Favorite mad doctors... How about:
1. Herbert West from the *Re-Animator* movies. He was one crazy and drivin' S.O.B.
2. Dr. Logan from *Day of the Dead*. Come on, he tried to train the living dead and fed them pieces of dead people he saved in a fridge.
3. Dr. Frankenstein from *Young Frankenstein*. I don't think I need to elaborate here.
—Jason

No question—Dr. Paul Carruthers (Bela Lugosi) from *The Devil Bat*. Goggles, shaving lotion, bats, One-Shot McGuire... how can it not make the top five!
—Mike

1. George Zucco in *The Mad Ghoul*. The brilliant mind twisted by love—it's the old bromide, but pulled off in grand style by Zucco, who makes poor David Bruce the ultimate dupe to his plans. Science be damned, this guy wants a roll in the hay with Evelyn Ankers, and if a few corpses get mutilated, a few folks get their hearts cut out, that's the price to be paid for love.
2. John Carradine in *Captive Wild Woman*. Unlike brother scientist Zucco, Carradine's only focus is scientific progress. We're still not sure what he's trying to prove with the animal glands. It's a very Dr. Moreau-like process, but there's no doubting Carradine's dedication or insane state of mind. Great stuff.
3. Onslow Stevens in *House of Dracula*. Stevens is one of the best noble men of medicine, transformed by a good deed. What scientist could resist finding out what makes Dracula, Larry Talbot and The Frankenstein Monster tick? Unlike Karloff's Dr. Niemann, Dr. Edelmen is a doctor with a sincere desire to help mankind. Of course everything goes wrong—you can't get mixed up with the Universal monsters without paying the price—but this is one of the last great gems of a performance from the classic Universal horror period.
4. Bela Lugosi in *The Return of the Ape Man* and *Bowery at Midnight*. *Return of the Ape Man:* One of Lugosi's straighter performances for Monogram—it doesn't have the goofy energy (or outcome) of *The Ape Man*, but it does show Bela in a serious mood doing serious (?) work in the old lab. Certainly not as colorful as Mirakle from *Murders in the Rue Morgue* or as gonzo as Dr. Vollin in *The Raven*, but this is a good, solid man-of-science turn for Lugosi, in one of the better Monogram/Sam Katzman flicks, and deserves some of the recognition other Lugosi movies already enjoy. *Bowery at Midnight*: Rather too similar to *The Human Monster*, this crime/horror flick has a better script and cast than some other Lugosi vehicles, and Wallace Fox punches the thing home. A nice turn from Bela as a doc with a split personality.
5. Boris Karloff in *Frankenstein 1970*. Why in the world *this* movie and *this* performance? Karloff's turns in the Columbia Mad Doctor series are all solid entertainments, *Black Friday* the same. He paid the price for tampering in *The Invisible Ray*

and there's nobody as hell-bent on revenge as Dr. Neimann, but Karloff is so over-the-top in this movie, just chewing the scenery to bits, that it amps the enjoyment level of this Howard Koch effort right to the ceiling. He made better movies (lots of 'em) and was better in them, but there's something wonderfully seedy about the movie and Karloff's approach that hits the right Saturday afternoon chord.

And Peter Cushing in *anything*.
—Courtney Joyner

1. Dr. Henry Frankenstein (Colin Clive, *Frankenstein/Bride of Frankenstein*): What can I say? This guy in the number one spot was an offer I couldn't refuse. Without a doubt, the Godfather of all the movie mad doctors!
2. Dr. Pretorius (Ernest Thesiger, *Bride of Frankenstein*): Tremendous evil, not to mention that zany haircut and white robe have become the epitome of the mad doctor. Pretorius is second only to Dr. Frankenstein. Just listen to Pretorius while conversing with Clive's Frankenstein... "You think I'm mad. Perhaps I am...Now think, what a world astounding collaboration we should be—you and I together!" He's simply meant to be on this list.
3. Jack Griffin aka the Invisible Man (Claude Rains, *The Invisible Man*): This was Rains' American film debut, and it came under some trying circumstances. After all, he was totally covered in bandages, and was almost forced completely to act with his voice. "Here we go gathering nuts in May on a cold and frosty morning...."
4. Dr. Bill Cortner (Herb Evers, 1962, *The Brain That Wouldn't Die*): What a romantic mad doctor this guy was. He so loved his fiancée, Jan (played by Virginia Leith), that he kept her severed head alive, after she was decapitated in a terrible auto accident. For most of the film, he searches for the perfect body to go with it. Now, if that's not love, I don't know what is?
5. Dr. Gustav Niemann (Boris Karloff, 1944, *House of Frankenstein*): The man who escaped from Neustadt Prison and tried to follow in Henry Frankenstein's footsteps certainly accomplished enough to warrant the number five spot on this list. And it was quite an ironic part with the character filling the mad doctor's shoes, and the actor portraying him being the one who played that mad doctor's famous creation in the first three *Frankenstein* films.
—Sam Borowski

In order of their appearance on the screen, the top five loony docs are, in my opinion:
1. Dr. Bohmer (*Ghost of Frankenstein*, Universal, 1942). As portrayed by Lionel Atwill, Bohmer, the junior partner of Dr. Ludwig Frankenstein, allows professional jealousy to push him over the edge. Thus, he transplants the wily Ygor's brain into the Monster with predictable chaotic consequences.
2. "Temporary Insanity" describes my next favorite mad doctor, Dr. Frank Mannering. Mannering (Patric Knowles) is a kind, compassionate and quite rational M.D. in *Frankenstein*

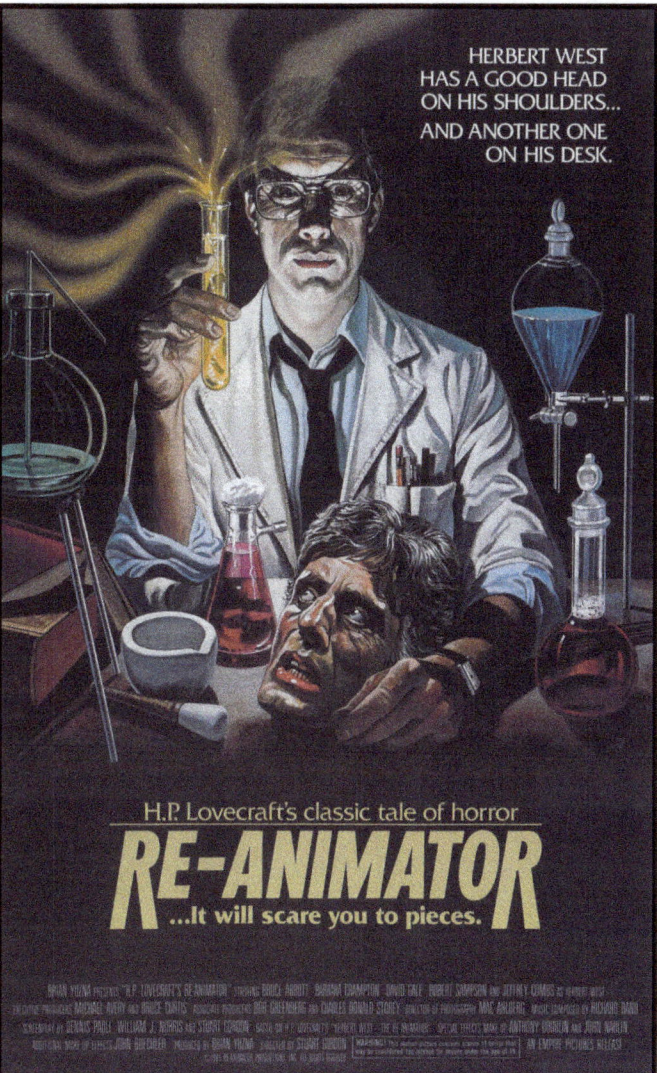

Meets the Wolf Man (Universal, 1943). Toward the end of the film, he completely looses it in a sudden mad desire to "see the Monster at its full strength." Wildly revving up the power to the Monster's electrodes, only the screaming and pleading of lovely aristocratic Ilsa Frankenstein (Ilona Massey) restores him to his senses, before the walls come tumbling down—quite literally.
3. Next, Dr. Andrew Forbes (George Zucco) is the primary care archeologist to a homicidal giant bird in PRC Pictures' *The Flying Serpent* (1946). Dr. Forbes' patient also happens to be an ancient Aztec god named Quetzalcoatl, who obligingly zaps those hapless folks who manage to annoy the not-so-good doc.
4. Fast forwarding nine years to Ed Wood's *Bride of the Monster*, Lugosi delivers the ultimate Bela "over the top" performance as Dr. Eric Vornoff. Driven from his homeland by those who, quite naturally, mistook his genius for madness, Bela pulls out all the stops. Only an atomic explosion (yes, an atomic bomb!) puts an end to this mad doctor's practice.
5. My fifth and final favorite mad doctor is Emil Zurich, as played by the ever-sinister Henry Daniell, in 1959's *Four*

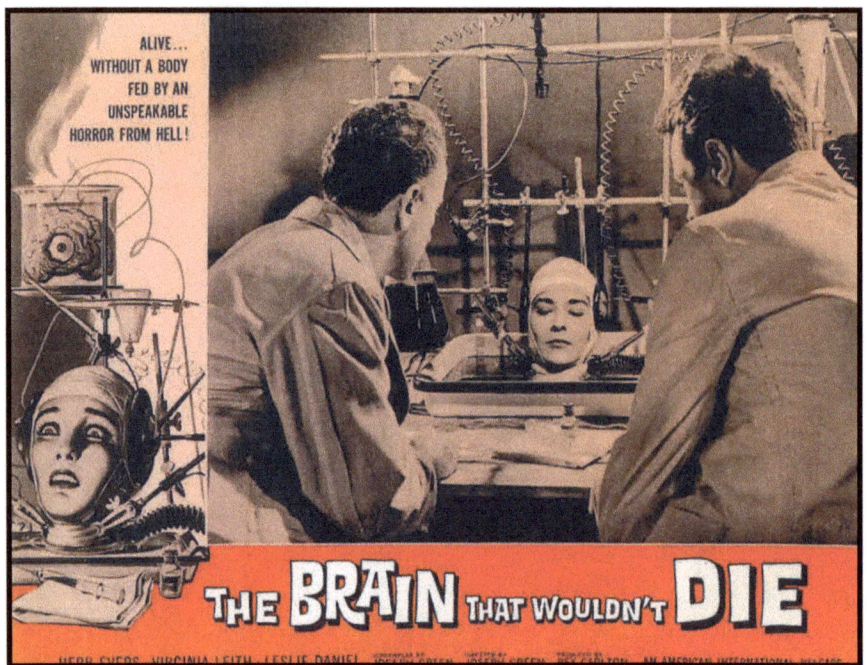

Skulls of Jonathan Drake, from Vogue Pictures. Dr. Zurich spends his considerable lifetime (200 years) removing and shrinking the heads of the unfortunate male members of the Drake family. Finally, Jonathan Drake figures a way to remove the doctor's shingle…permanently.
—Phil Bisson.

Mad Doctors in Movies:
1. Peter Cushing in Hammer's *Frankenstein* movie series
2. Vincent Price in the two *Dr. Phibes* movies
3. Colin Clive in the first two Universal *Frankenstein* movies
4. Basil Rathbone in *Son of Frankenstein*
5. Kenneth Branagh in *Mary Shelley's Frankenstein*
Honorable Mention—Fredric March in his Oscar-winning role in *Dr. Jekyll and Mr. Hyde*, Bela Lugosi in *Bride of the Monster* and Jeremy Irons in *Dead Ringers*.

Mad Doctors on Television:
1. Jack Palance as Dr. Jekyll (1969)
2. Harley Quinn (*Batman: The Animated Series* [and *Birds of Prey*])
3. Leonard Whiting as Dr. Frankenstein from *Frankenstein: The True Story*
4. Dr. Eric Lang (*Dark Shadows*)
5. Paracelsus (*Beauty and the Beast*)
—Jeff Thompson

Five favorite mad doctors:
1. Peter Cushing as Baron Frankenstein in *Frankenstein Must Be Destroyed*—In all six times Cushing played the role, never was he as ruthless or condescending as he was in this film. Like most mad doctors in cinema, he has but one single focus to be carried out despite any obstacles. In this case, to transplant the brain of an insane, dying colleague into another healthy body. Along the way he commits robbery, kidnapping, murder and even rape. Never was the Baron this unsympathetic (or delicious to the audience)!
2. Lionel Atwill as Dr. Rigas in *Man Made Monster*—This was the best of Lionel's mad doctor roles (the film also introduced Lon Chaney, Jr., to the horror genre). Atwill's bug eyes were right up there with the best of them (except for George Zucco). But nobody could match his leer, especially when he forcefully straps Anne Nagel to his lab table, intent on killing her with electricity. All of Atwill's roles were delightful, but here he shines (glows?).
3. As mentioned earlier, the eyes have it—and George Zucco has the eyes! My favorite of his roles is Professor Andoheb in *The Mummy's Hand*, but since that character isn't a mad doctor, I'll select Dr. Morris in *The Mad Ghoul*. Compared to some of his other portrayals, Dr. Morris was rather low-key, but his eyes still reflected the character's evil and lechery (lusting after Evelyn Ankers, despite her atrocious 1940s hairstyle)!
4. Jeffery Combs as Herbert West in *Re-Animator*—Herbert West is a great character: intense, pouting, sullen, surly, sardonic and brilliant. He is so enamored of his glow-in-the-dark re-agent that he fails to see its results. Every person or animal he brings back to life is outraged, murderous and destructive. West is oblivious to this unless he's defending himself from one of these corpses. He even ignores a naked Barbara Crampton.
5. Bela Lugosi as Dr. Vollin in *The Raven*—You really have to admire a guy who builds his own torture chamber and talks to a stuffed raven and bust of Pallas, spouting lines like "Poe, you are avenged!" (I didn't know Poe needed avenging.) Bela is cultured and maniacal. When he laughs at his prisoner Boris Karloff, he is *way* over the top. This is one of Bela's better roles and the one time he should have received top billing over Karloff.
—Gary Billings

1. Dr. Phibes—First of all, it's Vincent Price. Ya can't go wrong there. And second, ol' Phibesy was just so delightfully twisted and ingenious. All those clever ways to send his victims screaming to their graves. I could never wait to see his next little gimmick. Yeah, I gotta vote for ol' Doc Phibes, for sure.
2. Dr. Plato Zorba (from *13 Ghosts*)—While he may not be considered by some to be a mad scientist (since in the original—and best—movie, he was already dead), you have to consider him for a spot here. I mean, how cool is it to hunt ghosts….and even *capture* them. And then live right there in the same house with the spooks you captured?!! I mean,

wouldn't you think they'd be sore at you?! Yeah, he had to be nuts, all right. But ya gotta admire anyone who hunts ghosts for giggles, no? So dead or not, I gotta vote for Doc Zorba as a favorite whacked out scientist, even though I'm pretty sure not many will agree with me.

3. Herbert West—Oh, okay, so he's not one of the "oldies but goodies." He's still a Class-A psycho. Anyone who re-animates dead folks for fun is okay in my book. And he was always so deadpan serious about it! A delightfully delusional mad scientist. He's on *my* list.

4. Dr. Henry Frankenstein—In *any* incarnation, this guy has got to be on the list. No other mad scientist has popped up in the annals of horror as often as crazy Henry/Victor/The Baron. No matter who plays him, he'll always be way up there on the nutso scale. I mean, c'mon.... sewing parts of cadavers together and then using the ol' key on the kite trick to zap 'em to life? Wow. Yeah, he's mad as a hatter, all right.... and totally oblivious to the fact! Dr. Frankenstein goes on my list, too.

5. Dr. Henry Jekyll—Now this guy knew how to party! He creates a lively brew that brings out the animal in himself and then he goes and has his way with the ladies! He may be butt ugly, but he certainly woos the frillies off them, doesn't he? You just have to admire a guy who creates juice that can make him a dashing lover even if he has a face only a nearsighted mom could love. He may have been mad, but he definitely had some ideas of what's fun! He gets *my* vote!

6. Any mad scientist played by King Karloff! That says it all. If he were a mad scientist in a movie, that performance became a favorite of mine. Karloff was, is and always will be the king of the monsters and madmen! Long may he rest in peace, although he shall never be forgotten! Any scientist he played could both charm and give you the willies, all at the same time. Sorry to be vague on this one, but so it goes. Karloff made the role, not the other way around.
—Tom Detoro (aka "Renfield")

The mad doctors in my life are:
1. Dr. Frankenstein (Colin Clive)—Power obsessed. Playing God. Skulking through cemeteries.
2. Dr. Pretorius (Ernest Thesiger)—Out of his mind, not to mention he has that small, coffin-looking box full of miniature people.
3. Dr. Moreau (Charles Laughton)—He scared me to death… everyone scared me to death in this! Yet I'm still alive! I'm now the undead… good gosh! The House of Pain!
4. Baron Frank (Boris Karloff)—*Frankenstein 1970*. First Frankenstein movie I saw. I couldn't speak English yet, but was enthralled by Boris' voice! I would watch anything with

him in it! In *Frankenstein 1970* his creation was creepy since it was all bandaged up!
5. Dr. Gogol (Peter Lorre)—from *Mad Love*. He's obsessed!! "But I *must* have you!" Mad doctors are the scariest, because they take their time.
—Rose Solar

While it is difficult narrowing down a list to a top five from some many fine contenders, here is my top five list of the Greatest Mad Scientists of All Time:

1. Dr. Victor Frankenstein (Peter Cushing), whose series of movies still remains one of the finest horror series of all time. While the Byronic qualities remain essentially the same throughout the series, Cushing's Frankenstein does range from being fairly benign (in *Evil of Frankenstein*) to egregiously malignant (in *Frankenstein Must Be Destroyed*). Cushing's portrayal of world-weary doggedness in pursuit of his goal remains memorable, though ironically, it is his assistant in *Revenge of Frankenstein* that achieves the greatest success in his experiments.

2. Dr. Henry Frankenstein (Colin Clive) is still one of the screen's most memorable dreamers. His seems a fevered and tormented soul, despite his exaltation of knowing what it feels like to be God. Sadly, he never takes responsibility for his neglect of his creation, but it is hard to beat the one-two punch of *Frankenstein* and *Bride of Frankenstein*.

3. Dr. Bernardo (John Carradine) from *Everything You Wanted to Know About Sex But Were Afraid to Ask* remains one of the maddest mad scientists of all-time. Carradine was good at playing crazy medicos, but this Woody Allen-written send-up of the genre allows him to be totally unfettered and extremely funny. (Bernardo wants to create, for example, the world's largest diaphragm, to force a man to have sex with a large

loaf of bread, to measure the pulse rate of a woman being gang-banged by cub scouts. Masters and Johnson, eat your heart out).

4. Dr. Janos Rukh (Boris Karloff) from *The Invisible Ray* belongs up there. Karloff creates a character that is far better off in the laboratory than he is in dealing with people. Karloff limned many fine medical luminaries, but to me, Rukh is one of his most memorable, with the added bonus of his pairing with Bela.

5. Dr. Gogol (Peter Lorre) from *Mad Love* makes the final cut, beating out Lorre's amusing turns as Dr. Einstein, Dr. Lorantz and Dr. Adolphus Bedlo. Lorre's acting as Gogol isn't as caricatured as some of his later work, and it is a dazzling piece of acting. With eye movements and body language, Lorre conveys Gogol's obsession: love, frustration, exhaustion, madness and torment. This is one of horror's greatest *tour de force* performances, well worth savoring for Lorre's ability to create sympathy for a vindictive, bug-eyed creep.
—Dennis Fischer

My Five Ghastly Mad Scientists (And Five Runners-up):
1. John Dehner's decidedly loopy departure from slick-tongued villains, and instead he plays it strictly for shtick in *The Bowery Boys Meet the Monsters* (1954).

2. Narda Onyz is the sensually ripe over-the-top relative of Herr Frankenstein in *Jesse James Meets Frankenstein's Daughter* (1966).

3. Whit Bissell becomes the self-concerned dedicated scientist off his collective rocker in *I Was a Teenage Frankenstein* (1957).

4. Donald Murphy plays the smooth, venomous, handsome and classy do-it-his-way-or-no-way murderous scientist in *Frankenstein's Daughter* (1958).

5. John Hoyt as the pitiless live puppet master scientist, from *Attack of the Puppet People* (1958), who is god of his own cruel laboratory world, definitely one brick shy of a load here.

Runners-up:
6. Robert Evans is purely vicious as the evil, twisted psycho maniac in *The Fiend Who Walked the West* (1958). He does snivel when justice turns the tables.
7. Michael Gough as the arrogantly prissy doctor, who smirks most cowardly in his embrace of *Konga* (1961), at the finale.
8. Guy Rolfe's former haughty in-charge dominance is broken down, then sheer panic results from Oscar Homolka's torturous lies at the end of *Mr. Sardonicus* (1961).
9. Torin Thatcher's sadistic streak is turned to pure jelly as his sorcerer's bag of tricks won't save his bacon when he's on

the receiving end of fear, horror and death from *The Seventh Voyage of Sinbad* (1958).

10. Niall MacGinnis' cunningly crafty portrayal of evil starts to crumble when the tables are turned and the parchment is passed to him. He does a great warlock sprint and dash to try to save his skin, in true sniveler's fashion in *Curse of the Demon* (1957).

—William Wilkerson

1. Peter Cushing's performance as Baron Frankenstein from the Hammer Frankenstein series reveals Peter Cushing's portrayal of the Baron to be the most complex and consistently developed mad scientist in movies. When looked at consecutively, we have the evil obsession of *Curse of Frankenstein*, the in-disguise dedicated man of medicine in *Revenge of Frankenstein*, the emerging cynic of *Evil of Frankenstein*, the dashing romantic rogue of *Frankenstein Created Woman*, the almost bitter misanthrope of *Frankenstein Must Be Destroyed* and the aging and pathetic world-weary medical adventurer of *Frankenstein and the Monster from Hell*. Cushing has created a richness of character that is multi-layered—one of the most memorable horror film performances yet created.

2. Colin Clive's Dr. Frankenstein in *Frankenstein* and *Bride of Frankenstein*—Colin Clive's version of Dr. Frankenstein is more high-strung than Cushing's and also more one-dimensional, but Clive's obsession set the standards for other mad scientists to come. His wild-eyed cries of "It's alive" as he looks skyward, ranting and mumbling to himself, or his rude welcoming of human visitors to his secret watchtower,

including his bride-to-be, only demonstrates his fatalistic dedication to the world of science, daring to rob heaven of its secrets at any cost.

3. Pierre Brasseur as Dr. Genessiere in *Eyes Without a Face* (1960)—This haunting French horror thriller still mesmerizes with its rich black-and-white photography and fairy tale quality. We have a disfigured Edith Scob, wearing an ivory-white mask, literally floating around the mansion and nearby forest, as her obsessed and guilt-ridden doctor/father abducts young female victims, murders them and removes their faces in gruesome operations, attempting to restore his daughter's ravished features. Brasseur's performance is quietly evil—his non-expressive face and delicate way with his daughter contrasts to his perverse stalking of innocent young women—making him one of the more subtle mad scientists of movies.

4. Lionel Atwill in *Doctor X, Mystery of the Wax Museum, Murders in the Zoo* and *The Vampire Bat*—The bulky and steely-eyed Lionel Atwill, sometimes wearing thick glasses and maintaining a stoic face reinforced by a formal British voice, seems to be playing against type when he becomes one of the first actors to be stereotyped as a mad scientist (even becoming a red herring in *Doctor X*). Atwill's insanity, emerging at some pivotal point during each production, always seems to be revealed shockingly with the maximum of surprise, as his proper Brit persona is revealed to harbor raving passions just beneath the surface that seem to burst forth from him much as lava overflows an erupting volcano.

5. Bela Lugosi in *The Devil Bat, The Invisible Ghost, Return of the Apeman, Bride of the Monster*, etc.—Bela Lugosi, the best mad doctor of Poverty Row Hollywood, is so successful because of his unwavering dedication to his performance, even when cardboard sets ripple around him and the most unspecial effects threaten to sink any credibility the movie might possess. Supporting actors might seem stiff or over-emote, but the consummate professional Lugosi never delivers less than his best. And his megalomaniacal leanings often become the only reason to keep watching.

—Gary J. Svehla

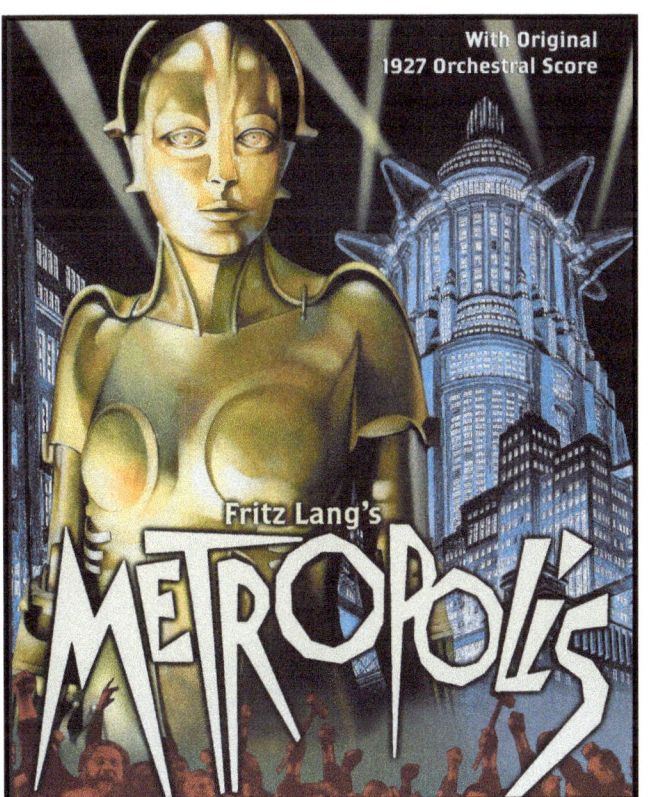

Karloff: The Maddest Doctor of All???
The Devil Commands vs. The Man Who Changed His Mind

Gary J. Svehla (**GS**) wrote (in *Midnight Marquee* 71/72) about the relative merits of recently DVD-released *The Man Who Changed His Mind* (1936; U.S. title: *The Man Who Lived Again*) and *The Devil Commands* (1941), little realizing that he would provoke a firestorm of controversy among the magazine's regular contributors. First Mark Clark (**MC**) and James J.J. Janis (**JJ**) started in on him. It wasn't long before Anthony Ambrogio (**AA**), Arthur Joseph Lundquist (**AJL**) and Steven Thornton (**ST**) joined the fray, by which time the debate moved off into some surprising directions. Luckily, Bryan Senn (**BryS**) was there to bring the discussion back to its beginnings. [*Spoiler alert*: If you don't want to know what happens at the end of *The Man Who Changed His Mind* or *The Devil Commands*, don't read this article!]

GS: As I wrote in my DVD review for the summer 2004 *MidMar*, I think people will over-react and over-praise the merits of *The Man Who Changed His Mind* simply because the film has been nearly lost. It does look gorgeous, but the soundtrack is thin and very, very hissy! You won't notice the hiss until now that I mentioned it, and now that's all you will hear.

Karloff is great, and his performance is one of his best. But compare the film to *The Devil Commands*. I prefer *The Devil Commands* because everyone in it lets his or her hair down and just rocks out. *The Devil Commands* is a superior B production. *The Man Who Changed His Mind* is a tad more formally Brit, pretentious and stiff upper lip. Also, one of *The Man Who Changed His Mind*'s major flaws is that, although during the course of the movie every major player gets to imitate some other major player, *Karloff does not*. When his character's mind is changed into another body, he dies before he has the chance to imitate anyone. And, as I said, *The Man Who Changed His Mind* is so *veddy* British. For me, *The Devil Commands* is the better film. I prefer Karloff's performance therein. It's more natural and haunting. It touches me emotionally. The vacant look on Karloff's face speaks volumes.

MC: *The Devil Commands* is very good but not quite as well executed, overall, as *The Man Who Changed His Mind*. *The Devil Commands*, generally, has a haggard look about it.

GS: I have to disagree here. Karloff's haggard look is the basis for a first-rate performance. First of all, let's compare directors: the superb B-film director Edward Dmytryk for *Devil*, Robert Stevenson for *Mind*.

JJ: Stevenson is a criminally underrated director. I'd put him up against Dmytryk—whose batting average fell precipitously in the 1950s. Not so Stevenson.

[Dmytryk's directing career from its commencement to 1959: *The Hawk* (1935), *Television Spy* (1939), *Emergency Squad* (1940), *Golden Gloves* (1940), *Mystery Sea Raider* (1940), *Her First Romance* (1940), *The Devil Commands* (1941), *Under Age* (1941), *Sweetheart of the Campus* (1941), *The Blonde From Singapore* (1941), *Secrets of the Lone Wolf* (1941), *Confessions of Boston Blackie* (1941), *Counter-Espionage* (1942), *Seven Miles from Alcatraz* (1942), *Hitler's Children* (1943), *The Falcon Strikes Back* (1943), *Captive Wild Woman* (1943), *Behind*

the Rising Sun* (1943), *Tender Comrade* (1943), *Murder, My Sweet* (1944), *Back to Bataan* (1945), *Cornered* (1945), *Till the End of Time* (1946), *So Well Remembered* (1947), *Crossfire* (1947), *Obsession* (1949), *Give Us This Day* (1949), *Mutiny* (1952), *The Sniper* (1952), *Eight Iron Men* (1952), *The Juggler* (1953), *The Caine Mutiny* (1954), *Broken Lance* (1954), *The End of the Affair* (1955), *Soldier of Fortune* (1955), *The Left Hand of God* (1955), *The Mountain* (1956), *Raintree County* (1957), *The Young Lions* (1958), *Warlock* (1959), and *The Blue Angel* remake (1959).]

[Stevenson's directing career from its commencement to 1959: *Happy Ever After* (1932), *Falling for You* (1933), *Tudor Rose* (1936), *The Man Who Changed His Mind* (1936), *The Two of Us* (1936), *King Solomon's Mines* (1937), *Non-Stop New York* (1937), *Owd Bob* (1938), *The Ware Case* (1938), *Young Man's Fancy* (1940), *Return to Yesterday* (1940), *Tom Brown's School Days* (1940), *Back Street* (1941), *Joan of Paris* (1942), *Forever and a Day* (1943), *Jane Eyre* (1944), *Dishonored Lady* (1947), *To the Ends of the Earth* (1948), *I Married a Communist* (1950, aka *Woman on Pier 13*), *Walk Softly, Stranger* (1950), *My Forbidden Past* (1951), *Johnny Tremain* (1957), *Old Yeller* (1957), and *Darby O'Gill and the Little People* (1959)—plus episodes of the TV series *Gunsmoke*, *The 20th Century-Fox Hour*, *Alfred Hitchcock Presents* (all 1955), and *Zorro* (1957).]

MC: Stevenson was a perfectly capable craftsman. In fact, until the emergence of Steven Spielberg, he was the top-grossing director of all time, thanks to his series of hit comedies made at Disney in the 1960s—things like *Mary Poppins*.

[Stevenson's unbroken streak of Disneyana, which began with the aforementioned *Johnny Tremain*, *Old Yeller*, and *Darby O'Gill*, lasted for almost 20 years: *Kidnapped* (1960), *The Absent-Minded Professor* (1961), *In Search of the Castaways* (1962), *Son of Flubber* (1963), *The Misadventures of Merlin Jones* (1964), *Mary Poppins* (1964), *The Monkey's Uncle* (1965), *That Darn Cat!* (1965), *The Gnome-Mobile* (1967), *Blackbeard's Ghost* (1968), *The Love Bug* (1968), *My Dog, the Thief* (1969, TV), *Bedknobs and Broomsticks* (1971), *Herbie Rides Again* (1974), *The Island at the Top of the World* (1974), *One of Our Dinosaurs Is Missing* (1975), and *The Shaggy D.A.* (1976).]

He's best remembered for those films, but Stevenson was a bit more versatile than those movies would suggest, and he displayed a flair for the Gothic with his 1944 *Jane Eyre* (starring Orson Welles). I'm not knocking Dmytryk, who was more of a stylist than Stevenson and made some superb films, but Stevenson was no hack.

Under Stevenson's direction, the supporting performances in *The Man Who Changed His Mind* are very strong. Not so *The Devil Commands*.

GS: I'll take the blacklisted stylist over the mainstream hitmaker any time! How can you say that the supporting performances are not as strong? The unsung Anne Revere as the charlatan spiritualist and Karloff's partner submits one of the finest female genre portrayals of the 1940s. She is

In America, *The Man Who Changed His Mind* **was retitled** *The Man Who Lived Again.*

utterly outstanding—creepy, strong-willed—and she always draws our attention to her. Revere's performance is simply fabulous—one waiting to be rediscovered.

MC: I don't know if I'd go *that* far, but she is certainly very good. Unfortunately, hers is the *only* memorable supporting performance in the film.

GS: The dimwitted Karl, played by Ralph Penney, is oddly charismatic. He's almost so real that his performance doesn't seem like a performance. But he is quirky and quite effective.

MC: I'm not nearly as impressed with Ralph Penney as you are.

AA: I wish they could have cast Lon Chaney, Jr., in that role. He would have been a natural, and it would have made the picture better—more iconic.

MC: Be honest, Anthony. You wish they had cast Lon Chaney, Jr., in everything! You probably would have been happy if they'd cast him in the Anna Lee role in *The Man Who Changed His Mind*!

Speaking of which, *The Man Who Changed His Mind* has *three* great supporting performances: Anna Lee, who's terrific as the heroine; Frank Cellier, as Haselwood, the self-serving

Dr. Julian Blair (Boris Karloff) looks haunted standing beside one of his seance-from-the-dead suits.

wealthy "philanthropist"; and Donald Calthrop as Clayton, the bitter old cripple who inherits Cellier's body. Cellier is even better once he begins playing Clayton-as-Haselwood.

GS: But, come on, does Karloff change his hairdo in *The Man Who Changed His Mind* like he does in *The Devil Commands*? The evolution of his coiffure from a slick combed-down look to weird curls actually makes the performance (as visual metaphor).

MC: You got me on that one.

ST: "And the Oscar for Best Hair Stylist goes to..."

GS: I find *Mind* a little too stiff and stuffy. *Devil* is fun all the way, with excellent supporting performances and superb direction by Dmytryk. It is my favorite Columbia Karloff. I can watch *The Devil Commands* over and over but *The Man Who Changed His Mind*, to me, does not lend itself to repeated viewings.

AJL: Need I add that Gary used to play *The Devil Commands* at Andover High at lunch times?

MC: I will grant that Karloff's character in *The Devil Commands* is much more sympathetic and, well, *Karloffian* than his character in *The Man Who Changed His Mind*. But *The Devil Commands* isn't my favorite Karloff Columbia mad-medico flick—that would be *The Man They Could Not Hang* (1939). However, I believe all three of these are very good films. I'm not sure any one is decidedly better than the other two. I've always liked *The Man Who Changed His Mind* best, *The Man They Could Not Hang* next and *The Devil Commands* third, but my margin of preference between each is small.

AA: Reluctantly leaving aside Lon Chaney, Jr., for a while, I wonder if it's not too far-fetched to suggest that *The Devil Commands* and *The Man Who Changed His Mind*, in different ways, foreshadow Karloff's later *The Sorcerers* (1967), directed by Michael Reeves, in which an old man (Karloff) and his wife (Catherine Lacey) practice mind control, à la *The Man Who Changed His Mind*, to vicariously, virtually feel younger people's experiences (sex, drugs, murder—this *was* the 1960s, after all)—and in which the woman, à la *The Devil Commands*, exerts greater and greater control over the man even as the experiment spins out of control.

The difference, though, is that, in *Sorcerers*, the experiment succeeds, and we get to see what happens. The thing I remember most upon first viewing *The Devil Commands* as a pre-teen is my frustrated disappointment that the movie ended before anything really happened. You know what I mean? Karloff is becoming more and more obsessed, setting up his experiment to talk to his dead wife; the preparations are becoming more and more elaborate and alarming, and—in the end—*nothing happens*. He gets interrupted. He dies. The end.

JJ: Karloff is *supposed* to be interrupted. He is about to go somewhere no one should go. If he got there, a whole can of worms would have been opened.

AJL: I go to the movies to see cans of worms opened.

ST: Yes, but Columbia couldn't afford a whole can of worms—only a night crawler or two.

AA: I'm with Arthur and the worms: That's why we watched these movies—to see the guy "tamper in things best left alone," to revel in the dire consequences, to be scared by resurrected dead bodies, vampires, spirits returning from the grave, etc. Not to be tantalized and frustrated. Does anybody else feel this way?

MC: Absolutely. If you want to be tantalized and frustrated, go to a nudie bar!

JJ: But the Invisible Man does *not* succeed in conquering the world. Frankenstein does *not* succeed in breeding a new race. Moreau does not succeed in creating the perfect humanimal and breeding it with a real human. Because there are things man must leave alone, and the Lord our God is a jealous God. One might as well criticize a Western because everyone rides horses...

AA: At least we got to see the Invisible Man *be* invisible. The movie didn't stop with the authorities arresting him just before he was about to take monocaine.

AJL: If *The Invisible Man* (1933) had worked like *The Devil Commands*, Griffin would have died just as his body first began to turn transparent, and the movie would have ended right there.

AA: Frankenstein *did* create a monster. The movie didn't stop with Elizabeth, Professor Waldman and Victor persuading him to give up his mad experiment and not throw the switch.

AJL: If *Frankenstein* (1931) had worked like *The Devil Commands*, Henry Frankenstein would have died just as his Monster first began to move, and the movie would have ended right there.

AA: And Moreau *did* create a whole bunch of manimals (and a womanimal) before everything came crashing down on him in the House of Pain.

AJL: If *The Island of Lost Souls* (1932) had worked like *The Devil Commands*, Moreau would have died just as his first animal began to mutate, ending the movie right there.

Anne Blair (Amanda Duff) is forced to wear one of the seance-from-the-dead suits, joining the small circle of corpses.

ST: Yet, in *The Devil Commands*, Karloff's character does come tantalizingly close to realizing his goal. You can actually make out his wife's voice before the final-reel tempest destroys his lab.

AA: And then it all ends. Why couldn't he have made contact? Why couldn't the plot have progressed from there (along lines similar to/different from *The Walking Dead* [1936], maybe)? Why did it have to end before it began?

AJL: Once more, Anthony, we are of a single mind. Or, should I say, a single brain. All of these former films dare to actually let their anti-heroes "tamper in things best left alone" and let us get to see them experience the consequences of their actions.

Or, put another way, those movies have the guts to actually open the can of worms that *The Devil Commands* politely won't.

GS: The same argument can be made, as I stated earlier, for *The Man Who Changed His Mind*. The movie ends before the Karloff character gets to mimic, his mind literally changed, another character. But the movie is what it is, and I accept that.

JJ: But that can of worms doesn't open because there are some things that man cannot do. If I remember correctly, the implication is that God basically said no. It is one thing to transgress against the laws of God and Man (and eventually pay the price). It is another thing entirely to storm the gates of Heaven... that probably goes a way toward explaining the film's title. Karloff may be a good man, but it is the devil that prompts him.

AJL: *The Devil Commands* goes nowhere because its jealous God slaps down its transgressor before he actually accomplishes anything. For me, that is a scriptwriter's cop-out, and the result is a very unsatisfying film, in spite of the abundant talents of all involved. Dmytryk's *Captive Wild Woman* (1943) has less on the ball, but actually delivers a helluva lot more.

GS: But, Arthur, *The Devil Commands* does deliver the goods. Karloff's character contacts the dead, and his experiments succeed. What about the major sequence where the machine is activated and all the corpses, dressed in their metallic best, all lean inward as the crazed Karloff stands at his command post? Things do happen here abetted by exciting visuals!

Dr. Claire Wyatt (Anna Lee) and Dr. Laurience (Boris Karloff)

Where could the movie have gone...what do you see as the next-stage cop-out? The film builds into the explosive storm *in the laboratory* and ends in a whirlwind of fury. My heavens, what more can a B programmer deliver, Arthur? This is an exciting, thrilling conclusion.

AJL: Oh, hell, Gary, Karloff is trying to break down the wall into the realm of the dead. Remember, he's got a whole tableful of corpses right in front of him. The newly liberated spirits of the dead would inevitably take refuge in the bodies, bringing them back to life. But the spirits, having been driven mad by the shock of death, would be screaming, pain-filled madmen. Maybe competing spirits would battle for possession of bodies. Karloff, perhaps assisted by the spirit of his dead wife, would be forced to open the celestial vortex again and send them back into death. There could even be some kind of moral about how the Earth is the home for the living, as Vera Brittain writes in her autobiographical account of WWI, *Testament of Youth*: "If the living are to be of any use in the world, they must always break faith with the dead."

The Devil Commands tempts us throughout the entire film with the idea that Karloff is going to pierce the barrier between the world of the living and the world of the dead. When he finally does, the movie simply ends. It is all build-up and no delivery. I demand delivery. I demand closure. I demand cans of worms be opened!

JJ: Oh—so Blofeld *should* have started WWIII in *You Only Live Twice* (1967)? So Ygor and Boehmer *should* have taken over the state in *Ghost of Frankenstein* (1942)? The Monster and the Bride *should* have mated and created a new race? Jekyll *should* have been successful in separating the evil in men's souls chemically? Regardless of how films may be today, one must take into account how films were then. There were certain places where one could go and then pay the price, and there were those where one paid the price for even the attempt. Lovecraft was big on the latter as well. There are simply places where men are forbidden to go. *The Devil Commands* is about one of those places. God said no. That is the crux of the film. One either goes with that, or one fails to comprehend the film. *The Walking Dead* is similar.

BryS: I disagree. *The Walking Dead* has, well, a walking dead. The film *begins* with Edmund Gwynne breaching the barrier he was not meant to breach, and then segues into the consequences/issues that arise after such a breach. *The Devil Commands* is all about the *striving* for such a breach (which

Dr. Laurience, now with wilder mad doctor hair, speaks with crippled Clayton (Donald Calthrop) and Haselwood (Frank Cellier).

is, in itself, a valid dramatic story, giving Karloff some choice emoting opportunities). But they are very different films in terms of structure. Oh, and *The Walking Dead* is a helluva lot better as well.

JJ: Except Gwynne, in *The Walking Dead*, breaches the barrier to find out what is on the other side and fails. The Lord our God *is* a jealous God.

AA: I know what you're getting at, James, but you misunderstand me, I think. The thrust of the Bond film is different from *The Devil Commands*. In *You Only Live Twice*, we have the forces of good confronting the forces of evil—lots of action and intrigue, etc.—and, in the end, the good guys win before the bad guy can destroy the world. Nothing dissatisfying or frustrating occurs there.

I'm afraid I don't understand your Jekyll/Hyde example because Jekyll *does* succeed in separating the evil in men's souls chemically. The film shows us what happens when Jekyll becomes Hyde—how evil can take over a man's body and soul and lead to devastation and ruin.

As for your other two examples—well, again, we'd already been given the sense of wonder and had a chance to wallow in supernatural satisfaction before *Bride of Frankenstein* and *Ghost of Frankenstein* came to an end. However, if the movies had been longer, and if the filmmakers would have deigned to show it, it would have been really interesting to see what would happen in a state ruled over by a mad (or at least very cranky) scientist and a Monster with the brain of a vengeful hunchback. Ditto a world of little monsters.

I understand that the "limits" established in the Golden Age were different and probably more narrow than they later became. I agree that sometimes the moral of a movie prevents Man from Tampering in God's Domain.

ST: Good points, Anthony. I've long felt that classic horror was the film genre most obsessed with God and morality, in spite of the many times it flirted with blasphemy.

AA: James mentions *Walking Dead*, as I did, and that's certainly the message in the end. However, at least we get to *see* Karloff as the walking dead, an inadvertent avenging angel of death, before the finale.

AJL: *The Devil Commands*' ending is where the movie should *start*. All it would take would be a screenwriter who was not afraid of actually exploring the ideas he brings up.

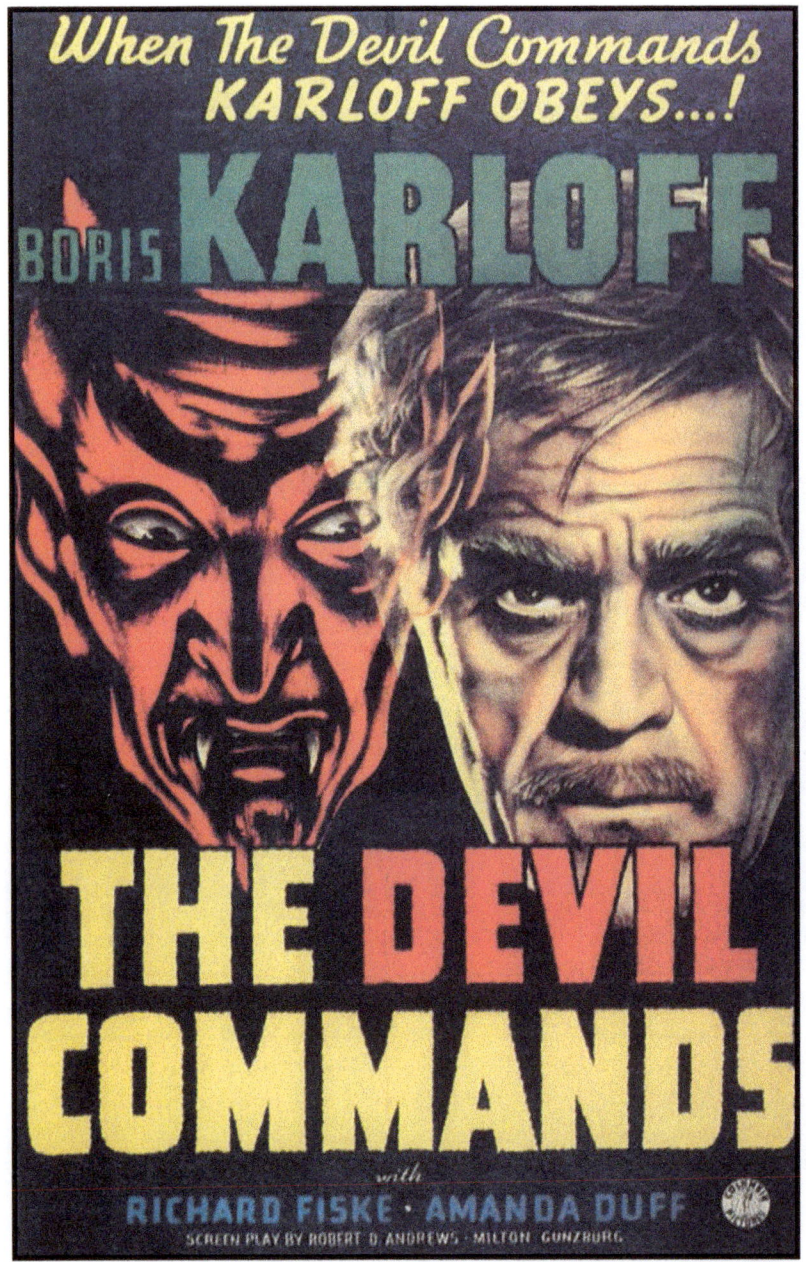

GS: No, no, no! Arthur, the focus in *The Devil Commands* is upon the scientist, his transformation from kind, nurturing husband to obsessed, deadly scientist who will violate any code to bring his dead wife's spirit back. The radical change in appearance (not just hair styles) Karloff undergoes only reinforces the point. This movie is character driven and is about how one's scientific obsessions can turn him evil. The movie is not about the product of his experiments. The movie's ending is satisfying, to me, because we clearly see how the altruistic Karloff character is destroyed, from within, having been seduced by the dark side. The plot is almost Shakespearean in structure.

BryS: Very convincing argument, Arthur. *The Devil Commands*' ending is indeed an abrupt letdown. But the film is not a total loss, due to its macabre topic and creepy atmosphere (and Karloff, of course). But yes, it could have (and *should* have) been a helluva lot more.

AJL: We are in complete agreement. I never said *The Devil Commands* was a total loss. Otherwise, I'd never be able to watch it to the end. It just lacks that zing at the finish that would carry it over into mythology. Movies with a helluva lot less to offer, like *The Unearthly* or *Invasion of the Saucer Men* (both 1957), manage in their final moments to give truly haunting spins on their central ideas and almost make the films worth sitting through.

For that matter, *Bride of Frankenstein* doesn't go on very long after the creation of the She-Monster, but in that short time it manages to touch all bases satisfyingly.

ST: *The Devil Commands*' script may be no great shakes, but this movie delivers the goods in terms of atmosphere far more effectively than most B movie programmers of the era. Plus it has a couple of very fun performances.

Captive Wild Woman (1943), on the other hand, always struck me as one of the least entertaining of the Universal Bs. Even with the presence of Carradine and some lively stock footage, this film seems dull as dishwater to me. I've never understood the minor cult surrounding it. Enlighten me, Arthur. What is it about this film that works for you?

AJL: Well, first, just in terms of comparison with *The Devil Commands*, I'd probably agree that *The Devil Commands* is perhaps better put-together technically than *Captive Wild Woman*. However, *The Devil Commands* is one of that breed of movies that makes me climb the walls, a movie that promises the world and then declines to deliver.

Captive Wild Woman, however, is about a mad scientist who wants to transform an ape into a woman. The movie goes on to present that very event and runs a few variations on the idea before it ends. Had *Captive Wild Woman* been structured like *The Devil Commands*, we would have ended up with something like *Sssssss* (1973), which is another film that makes me climb the walls, because we spend the whole damn picture waiting for the guy to get transformed into a snake, and, when he finally does, the movie suddenly terminates.

So that is why I'd rather sit through competent B-movie *Captive Wild Woman* rather than more-than-competent B-movie *The Devil Commands*.

Now, just in terms of itself, *Captive Wild Woman* does have a wonderful performance by John Carradine. In my article about the Paula the Ape Woman series, published years ago in *Midnight Marquee* and entitled "Universal's Poverty Row," I went on at length about a wonderful scene between Carradine and Fay Helm, where Carradine shows a lot of subtlety and a delicious sense of evil. Acquanetta is pretty if fairly vapid, and the rest of the cast is just adequate.

Captive Wild Woman's main attraction for me is that it is not just a gland movie (*The Monster Maker* [1944]), not just a brain transplant movie (*Ghost of Frankenstein*) and not just an ape movie (*White Pongo* [1945]), but a gland-transplant, brain-transplant, ape movie with deliberate sex appeal. The film splices together all four of the ways in which pulp writers pondered the question of human identity, after Darwin made us question whether we are divinely different from the animals. If its threads never really add up, at least they are there to play in our imaginations, as we remember the film (which for me accounts for much of my enjoyment of any movie). And in my case at least resulted in an unpublished gland-brain-ape novelette.

JJ: *The Devil Commands*, *Captive Wild Woman*: For the record. I like both.

MC: You must have skipped *Jungle Woman* (1944) and *Jungle Captive* (1945), then!

ST: Truthfully? I'd put them all on the same rung of the ladder—ground level.

AJL: Well, *Jungle Woman* is in a jaw-dropping basement all its own.

MC: *Captive Wild Woman* has that wild-and-woolly, anything-goes mentality going for it (sort of like a Silver Age DC comic book), an enjoyably over-the-top performance by Carradine and a hilariously inept one from Acquanetta. It's silly as all get-out, but it moves fast and is quite a bit of fun if you're in the right mood. *Jungle Woman*, however, is probably the dreariest, most lifeless hunk of junk Universal released during the 1940s. *Jungle Captive* recaptures some of the loopy fun of the original. It's passable.

JJ: I like all three Paula Dupree movies. I do not understand how anyone who professes affection for Ingmar Bergman or *Grand Illusion* (1937, the illusion being that anything is actually happening) can criticize the Ape Woman trilogy.

MC: Funny. I can easily understand how someone who enjoys *Jungle Woman* might not be able to grasp the appeal of Bergman and Renoir.

JJ: *I demand a Dupree DVD set now!* I would be willing to do the commentary. Besides, in the bad-Universal sweepstakes, as long as the 1941 *The Black Cat* exists, everything else is just an also ran…

AA: You're just jealous because the 1941 *Black Cat* has a better cast than all the Ape Woman films combined.

JJ: Two words, Anthony: Hugh Herbert.

AA: If only Lon Chaney, Jr., had played the Broderick Crawford part in *The Black Cat*!

GS: Arthur, your suggested extended ending for *The Devil Commands* would make a fine movie, but, within the confines of a B programmer, could it be accomplished in another 15-20 minutes or so? If we had to cut out stuff from the beginning, we would lose a lot, including much of the Karloff character's disintegration—which, to me, is the soul of the entire production. *The Devil Commands* is not really plot driven; it's character driven. If the movie went over 90 minutes, it would no longer be a B production. So we might have to sacrifice a fine Karloff performance in order to incorporate more plot. Would that be the best choice to make here? *I don't think so!* By allowing the screenwriter to open and explore his can of worms, something more important artistically would be lost.

AJL: The plot I suggested was just to illustrate that I could off the top of my head come up with a more satisfying climax using devices that the screenplay had already set up. Any person with imagination could create a more interesting climax.

It has been too long since I've seen *The Devil Commands* to remember anything in detail except my profound sense of being let down by the screenwriter. If the film went somewhere (anywhere) after its present climax and managed to stay 90 minutes long, we'd still have 90 minutes of Boris Karloff creativity, so I tend to doubt that anything would be lost.

Finally, may I suggest that this discussion is probably the most attention anybody has paid to *The Devil Commands* in decades. If the movie offered more, that would not be the case. Hell, if the movie ended with stock footage from *Dante's Inferno* (1935), we would have been talking about it for years.

GS: So Arthur, you admit you haven't seen *The Devil Commands* in ages! About your charge that the film hasn't received much attention in print in the past decade or so, Michael Price does a chapter on the Columbia Mad Doc series

Mrs. Walters (Anne Revere), a woman who claims she can communicate with the dead, begins to dominate the guillible Dr. Blair.

Dr. Julian Blair (Boris Karloff) and Anne Blair (Amanda Duff)

in his revised and definitive *Human Monsters* (Midnight Marquee/Luminary Press, 2004). Don Leifert did an article on them in *Video Review*. And I know I have read several articles on them in magazines within the past 15 years. With all the ink given Monogram, PRC, Universal, and all the rest, the time is ripe to rediscover this quartet of Karloff gems. The debate should be over which entry is the best: *The Devil Commands*, *The Man They Could Not Hang*, *Before I Hang* (1940) or *The Man with Nine Lives* (1940).

But the reason these films have not been discussed in print very often is because of their unavailability on home video. Too many people, like Arthur, remember the film from the dusty past of their memory, not from the definitive home-DVD release. I seem to be forced into the position of over-praising the film... I constantly state it is a B production (which *The Walking Dead* is technically *not*, and of course *Dead* is the superior movie). I happen to enjoy *The Devil Commands* because of two stellar performances, mood, creative photography and an involving plot. To me, a movie should be judged by what it *is* and *not* what each individual wishes it could have been. That is more wish fulfillment than film criticism. The sequence where Karloff's wife is killed is emotionally devastating, and the movie offers big bangs for the buck.

MC: I agree with this whole-heartedly.

GS: I don't see its abrupt ending as a screenwriter cop-out. For me, the film satisfies.

MC: Yes: Overall *The Devil Commands* satisfies. It's a good film! I believe the story ends where it does, as it does, mostly because Dmytryk and company didn't have money to do anything more elaborate.

By the way, Karloff also undergoes a hairdo change in *The Walking Dead*!

GS: I cannot argue and defend all its faults because it is a B production. (I love *The Devil Bat* [1940], but, if I spoke about the film's logic, special effects and hilarious performances— well, I wouldn't love that film as much as I do.) We have to give our beloved Bs some slack! *The Devil Commands* ("and Karloff obeys," as the merchandising made clear) is not just a film about a scientist who delves into God's domain and gets shut out; it is a film about how far a dedicated scientist and husband will go to keep his dead wife's spirit alive,

Boris Karloff as Dr. Laurience, stooped over and wild-eyed, has a captive audience in his grip.

and what depths he will plumb to Not Let Her Go. Thus, it is one of the more romantic-themed horror movies, and the deterioration of Karloff's sanity (symbolized by his radical hairdo change) from the first half to the second half makes this Karloff performance a true gem! It's like Karloff from *Black Friday* (1940) is merged with Janos Rukh from *The Invisible Ray* (1936), all within one movie.

AA: Well, while we were all debating, I *finally* finished watching *The Devil Commands* the other day (loaned to me by the courteous, erudite and thoughtful Steve Thornton). Here's my thought for a re-edit: If they had started the movie about a half-hour into the picture—at the point where the sheriff comes to the cliffside manor and questions the housekeeper, they could have extended the story beyond the almost-got-in-touch-with-his-wife-but-then-he-dies ending. With a few further lines of expository dialogue between the housekeeper and the sheriff, everything that came before could have been explained, and the story could have gone on from there. The only thing that *maybe* we would have lost by this approach was the loving relationship depicted between Karloff and his soon-to-be-dead wife in the early scenes (but this could have been remedied by a brief flashback somewhere else in the picture). Then we could have concentrated on the strange relationship between Karloff and the medium (what is the power that she wields over him? what kind of favors [sexual?] does she demand of him for her cooperation?) *and* we could have seen what happens *after* Karloff succeeds in contacting his wife. Since it turns out that his daughter is the *true* medium between him and his wife, what would happen if his wife begins to speak through and possess his daughter? Now, there's a kink worthy of a Lewton movie. Think Columbia could have pulled it off?

AJL: Only if they'd had the will, wit and imagination to try.

GS: But omitting the first third of the movie and creating a new, final third, *The Devil Commands* would not have been the same film, and by sacrificing the film's major focus, the transformation of Karloff's character, plot would have been stressed over characterization, thus destroying the film's major strength. Why not end *Casablanca* (1942) having Bogart and Bergman fly away together or have Bogart's detective play the fool and "take the fall" for the vile villainess at the end of *The Maltese Falcon* (1941)? Talk about opening a can of worms!

If I Only Had a Brain !!!
by Steven Thornton

The brain—a miracle of creation. With its highly selective ability to synthesize thought, emotion and complex motor functions, this incredibly organized collection of synapses and sensors is arguably the most awe-inspiring facet of the noble human animal.

Sounds like the perfect subject for a horror film!

In the 1940s, as horror cinema was walking the precarious tightrope between Gothic fantasy and scientific plausibility, filmmakers routinely pushed the envelope of available medical technology to provide their audience with thrills and chills anew. Blood transfusions, spinal fluid injections, glandular treatments—you name it, they utilized it, all in an attempt to add a jolt of fission to their latest matinee monstrosities. But no medical procedure was exploited as frequently or with as much cockeyed conviction as those involving the human brain.

Transplanted, transferred and transmuted, brains were swapped around 1940s horror films like cookies at a bake sale. A natural complement to the mad doctor motif seen in so many movies of that decade, the exchange of brains became the ultimate cinematic expression of man's efforts to circumvent the laws of nature. It is interesting in retrospect to note how much of this on-screen research work was written off as being "mad," "crazy" or just plain "screwy," in spite of the fact that it was more often than not based on quite reasonable motivations. Some of this reaction is presumably a reflection of our culture's discomfort with the rapidly accelerating pace of scientific and medical discovery, just as some can undoubtedly be attributed to the rumored "research" that was taking place in Hitler's concentration camps. In either case, the prevailing opinion of the time was that the brain was sacred ground—one of the final realms of the physical world that "man should leave alone."

Universal's 1931 *Frankenstein* was of course an important influence on this emerging sub-genre. Setting the standard, as it did for so many other aspects of cinema horror, this legendary film demonstrated the dramatic possibilities of brain switching gone awry. Going off on a discernible tangent, 1936's *The Man Who Lived Again*/aka *The Man Who Changed His Mind*, a Karloff vehicle produced in England, dealt with the transference of consciousness from one body to another. But by far the most significant catalyst for the predominance of brain switcheroos during the upcoming era was the work of Curt Siodmak. Author of the sci-fi novel *Donovan's Brain* and screenwriter for countless Universal horror films, Siodmak's contribution was instrumental in helping to shape the cinema of the fantastic during the "heady" days of the Second World War.

The horror films of the 1940s were markedly different from their Depression-era equivalents. Released against a backdrop of economic calamity and impending world conflict, the classic horrors of talking cinema's first decade pioneered a deep and haunting approach. But the chillers of the 1940s exhibited a decidedly less ambitious agenda. Denied the generous budgets and production polish evident in the films of horror's first wave, these genre entries scored their entertainment value

Ellen Drew is the victim of the monstrous gorilla, in this lobby card shot.

primarily by focusing on the lowest common denominator. Sophisticated storytelling, not surprisingly, was supplanted in favor of wild and woolly plots, stock characterizations and a notable level of weirdness inherent in their basic conceptions. Brain meddling was seen as a relatively inexpensive and expedient way to keep the squeamish factor at acceptable levels. After all, what could be more unnerving than the sight of a human brain free-floating in a laboratory beaker?

But let's not get ahead of ourselves.

As the new decade dawned, Universal Studios once again led the way. *Black Friday* (1940) was a curious amalgam of the horror and crime genres with a brain transplant featured prominently for good measure. While not the most sublime of the Karloff/Lugosi pairings, the film is representative of the scaled-down thrillers that would soon become the decade's norm. And as an introduction to our primer on brain transplants, it proves to be highly instructive.

Black Friday's peppy story line starts off in fifth gear and never slackens. When small-town college professor George Kingsley (Stanley Ridges) is run down by a speeding automobile, trusted friend and crackerjack surgeon Dr. Ernest Sovac (Boris Karloff) is forced to perform a partial brain transplant to save his life. Sovac's initial motives, to keep his friend alive while advancing the cause of science, are honorable enough. But when Sovac discovers that the donor who commandeered the runaway vehicle, crime boss Red Cannon, left behind a secret stash of a half million dollars, he begins to speculate on the extent to which the transplanted Cannon personality might still be intact.

Convalescing at his home, Kingsley begins to exhibit some of the gangster's instability and fits of uncontrollable rage. Sovac, taking note of his patient's unstable condition, prescribes a journey to New York City, which he hopes will rekindle the dormant criminal memories. Immersed in the intoxicating Big Apple environment, Kingsley displays further flashes of his alter ego's behavioral patterns, especially when he checks into the hotel suite that served as Cannon's secret hideaway. As depicted by *Black Friday*'s shooting script, brain grafting results in a Jekyll and Hyde persona, with each half struggling to dominate the whole.

Kingsley's condition continues to deteriorate as he absorbs repeated exposure to Cannon's haunts. Troubled by his

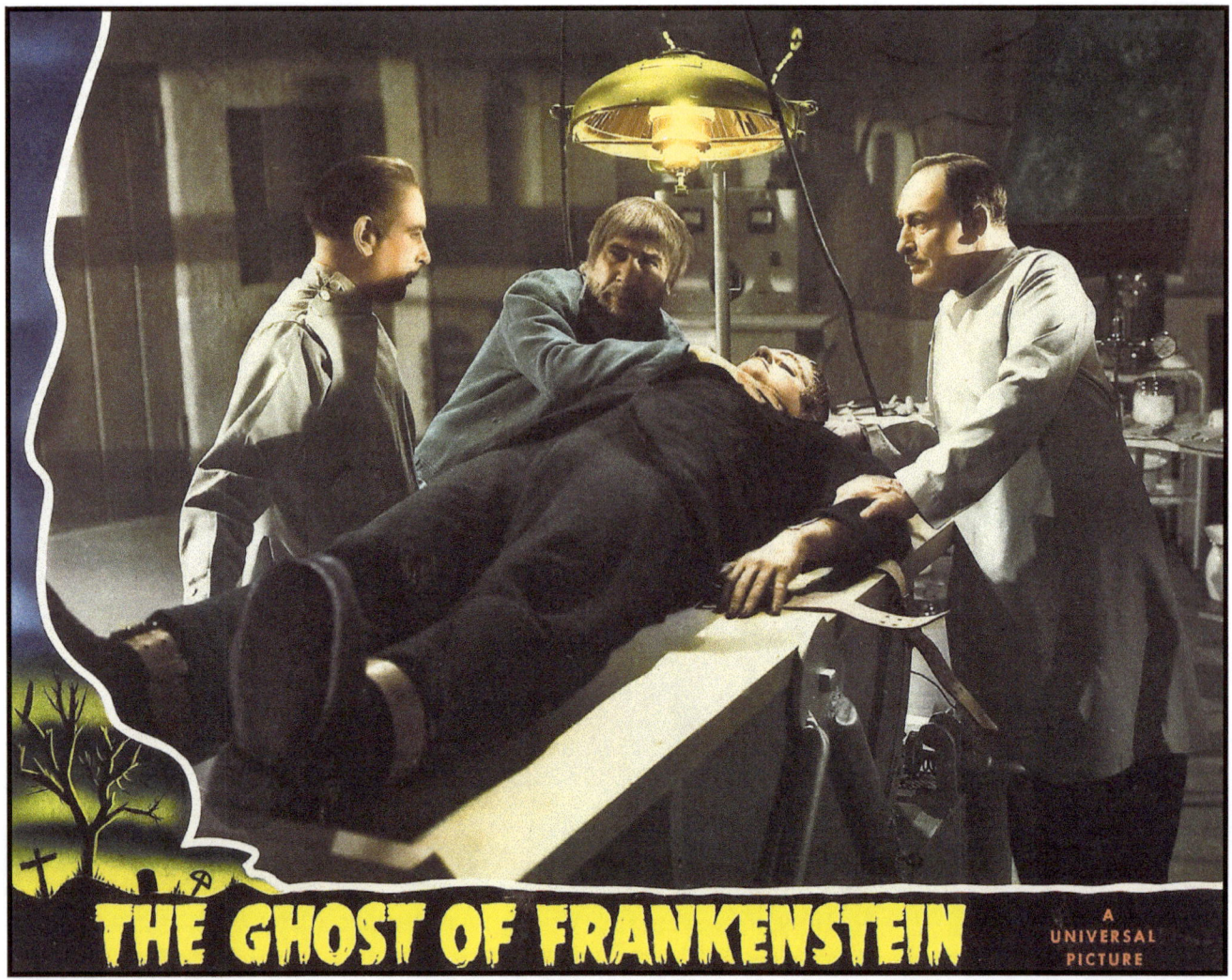

Credric Hardwicke (Dr. Frankenstein), Bela Lugosi (Ygor), Lon Chaney, Jr. (Monster) and Lionel Atwill (Dr. Bohmer)

recognition of former gang members and nightclub chanteuse Sunny (lovely Anne Nagel), the ailing professor succumbs to a blistering headache and a restless, dream-filled sleep. Going for broke, Sovac recites a litany of Cannon's cohorts in hopes of pushing the professor over the edge. To Sovac's amazement, the ploy is successful— Kingsley now takes on the physical and mental characteristics of the notorious crime king. Throughout the remainder of the film, this personality shift continues, with Kingsley morphing into Cannon at the wail of a police siren, then reverting back when his psychic storm (and the latest round of murders) has abated.

Black Friday is something of a redheaded stepchild in the Universal horror cycle due to its cosmopolitan setting and odd mix of criminal and horror elements. The film's reputation also suffers due to the woeful miscasting of Bela Lugosi as rival gangster Marnay. (As all good horror fans know, *Black Friday*'s original casting sheet pegged Lugosi in the Sovac role, with Karloff portraying Kingsley/Cannon. Karloff, reportedly unsure of his ability to convincingly portray a gangster, instead opted for the more conventional mad doctor role.) But by discounting this film, horror fans cheat themselves out of a fine performance by Stanley Ridges as the film's victim of "skullduggery." Aided by a simple but effective Jack Pierce makeup job, Ridge's character transformation is amazingly convincing; on first viewing, it is indeed hard to believe that the two performers are one and the same. Featuring brisk direction by Arthur Lubin and a loopy (but fun) plot line, *Black Friday* set the standard for a decade of brain-based thrillers yet to come.

Paramount's *The Monster and the Girl* (1941) has received much attention in the genre press lately as a neglected B-movie gem. With its hard-edged, urban atmosphere and unrelenting black tone, it is indeed a smart little entry in that sparsely populated category, the horror noir. Yet another overlooked aspect of this film is its earnest depiction of human-to-animal brain transference, a plot gimmick that could have easily toppled over into absurdity.

The story is centered on the misadventures of Susan Webster (Ellen Drew), whose dreams of the big city turn into a nightmare of forced prostitution. When brother Scott (Phillip Terry) attempts to discover her whereabouts, the crime mob that employs Susan has him framed on a murder charge and

Ilona Massey (Baroness Frankenstein), Patric Knowles (Mr. Mannering), Lon Chaney, Jr. (Larry Talbot), Bela Lugosi (Monster)

he is quickly sent to the electric chair. Horror film justice raises its twisted little head in the person of Dr. Perry (George Zucco), who receives official permission to use Scott's brain in an untried scientific experiment. Before the young man's corpse is cold, Perry is seen carting it off to his laboratory workshop, where the still-fresh brain is popped into the noggin of a full-grown gorilla.

Zucco's Dr. Perry is one of the more rational brain researchers of this decade, although his goal of helping to speed the path of evolution seems a tad overzealous. In any case, the procedure works far better than expected; prompted by the memory of Scott's trumped-up conviction, the ape escapes and begins to embark upon a very human plan of revenge. One by one, the prosecutor and gang members who helped seal Scott's fate are tracked down and bumped off, fulfilling his courtroom promise, "You'll get yours…all of you!"

In addition to its solemn, doom-laden atmosphere, a good deal of *The Monster and the Girl*'s effectiveness stems from its simian transplant recipient, played by a costumed Charles Gemora. With a long-suffering frown limned across his sad-eyed simian kisser, Gemora conveys convincingly the panic and confusion of doomed Scott Webster. Through body language alone, he also manages to communicate recognizable and sympathetic emotions behind the gorilla exterior. The acts of murder that the creature commits are likewise an enticing mix of human cunning and brute animal strength, with the ape (colorfully nicknamed the "Mangle Murderer" by the press) crashing through a window, plunging from a broken tree branch and, in one memorable shot, skulking through a hotel window to finish off its intended victim. At film's finale, when Susan comes face to face with the dying animal, its eyes and body language seem to cry out a silent but perceptible "Why?"

The Monster and the Girl will probably always be overlooked due to the absence of a certifiable marquee name. Zucco contributes little more than a walk-on and, while sharp-eyed film fans might spot Edward Van Sloan and Onslow Stevens in bit parts, most of the film revolves around Drew, Terry and the parade of character actors, who man the film's white slavery ring (Robert Paige, Paul Lukas, Joseph Calleia, et al.). But *Monster and the Girl* does deliver the goods in a

Reel Mad Doctors

Boris Karloff (Dr. Niemann) and J. Carrol Naish (Daniel) discover the ice-cave buried Frankenstein Monster.

pleasing manner, making one wish that Paramount were a more frequent visitor to the realm of the horror film. Satisfying too is the film's thoughtful and relatively serious attitude toward human/animal brain sharing, in spite of its potentially risible implications. For a subject that would eventually become the equivalent of a cinematic knock-knock joke, such an approach is a welcome revelation.

Universal's *Frankenstein* series is so familiar to fans of vintage horror that a lengthy analysis would likely risk triggering a villager uprising of our very own. But a quick recap of the later sequels in this venerable monster franchise confirms the studio's reliance upon brain transplants as a reliable plot catalyst. In addition, Universal's shifting treatment of the subject mirrors the genre's attitude toward brain swapping as a whole.

Things start off promisingly enough with 1942's *Ghost of Frankenstein*. Esteemed physician Ludwig Frankenstein (Sir Cedric Hardwicke), who specializes in "diseases of the mind," attempts to atone for his father's misdeeds by transplanting a healthy brain into the skull of the Frankenstein Monster (played on this one and only occasion by Lon Chaney, Jr.). His good works are thwarted, however, when ultra-ambitious assistant Dr. Bohmer (Lionel Atwill, who chews the scenery in splendid fashion) substitutes the cerebral matter of devious Ygor (Bela Lugosi). The end result is a power-hungry monster that speaks with Ygor's salient Slavic accent but (curiously) does not inherit any other of the donor's physical traits. Screenwriter W. Scott Darling, working from an original concept by Eric Taylor, continues to promote the "plug and play" approach to brain surgery, ignoring the need for lengthy convalescence. One novel feature of this movie does stand out—the Monster's sudden blindness, due to an unforeseen blood type mismatch. Such an unexpected development is a frank acknowledgment that the process might not be as foolproof as it is usually depicted.

Universal's next entry in the series, 1943's *Frankenstein Meets the Wolf Man*, is surprisingly light on the gray matter machinations in spite of a screenplay by brain transplant auteur, Curt Siodmak. Even the chronic blindness of the Ygorstein Monster is conveniently overlooked, suggesting that some sort of spontaneous adaptation has occurred. (Mavens of the series would quickly point out that references to the monster's affliction were included in the film's original shooting script. But since these scenes were expunged to the cutting room floor, and since the concept of a sightless Monster is never mentioned in future sequels, one is forced to chalk it up to the remarkable recuperative powers of Frankenstein's Creation.)

As if to make up for the prior film's omission, the next entry, *House of Frankenstein* (1944), is perhaps the most transplant-happy film in the entire canon. Self-schooled sawbones Dr. Niemann (Boris Karloff) is first observed contemplating the optimal method for placing a man's brain into the head of a dog, an exercise for which he, not surprisingly, landed in prison. Determined to follow in the footsteps of his idol Dr. Frankenstein, Niemann later promises to perform corrective surgery on posture-challenged Daniel (J. Carrol Naish) and lycanthropic Larry Talbot (Lon Chaney, Jr.), if they will help him locate the legendary medico's secret journals. Niemann's moment of personal triumph comes when he tracks down old nemeses Ullman and Strauss (Frank Reicher and Michael Mark), with plans to pop the gray matter of the former into the Frankenstein Monster, while giving the latter the brain of the Wolf Man. (One is tempted to suggest that this would only result in providing a new torso for the ever-suffering Talbot. But, whatever!) Sure enough, the intended victims are soon lying in Niemann's operating theater, their cerebellums floating in jars like so many pickled pigs' feet. Unfortunately, the doctor's "brainy" plans progress no further; his last-reel resuscitation of the Frankenstein Monster only helps to ensure a speedy end to both the film and his lofty but somewhat undisciplined ambitions.

Continuing the studio's on-again, off-again pattern, *House of Dracula* (1945) features little in the way of brain manipulation, save for Dr. Edelmann's (Onslow Stevens) attempt to use a special plant extract to reshape the cranial cavity of chronically cranky Larry Talbot (Chaney, Jr., of course). Of greater interest to budding neurologists is the series finale, 1948's *Abbott and Costello Meet Frankenstein*, in which Dracula (Lugosi) and femme fatale Dr. Sandra Mornay (Lenore Aubert) conclude that child-like Wilbur Gray (Lou

Jane Adams (Nina), Lon Chaney, Jr. (Larry Talbot), Onslow Stevens (Dr. Edlemann) and Glenn Strange (Monster)

Costello) would be an ideal brain donor for the titular monster. "He will obey you like a trained dog," promises Mornay, greatly overestimating their subject's mental capabilities. The operation nearly comes to pass (interestingly enough, without the use of ether or any other anesthetic), but in true Universal fashion, things go to hell before Costello is subjected to the final cut. A pity too—one was almost looking forward to the sight of the fondly remembered Monster wailing his arms incessantly and exclaiming, "Hey, Abbott!!!"

In retrospect, Universal's various Frankenstein wannabes tally an alarmingly low batting average in attempting to realize their scientific goals. Tripped up by secondary distractions, uncooperative assistants or just plain bad luck, these backroom surgeons followed the footsteps of their spiritual mentor more closely than they could have ever imagined. For serious students of brain surgery, these films amply demonstrate the pitfalls of life on the (scalpel) edge.

When it comes to horror film absurdity, it is difficult to top Monogram. A frequent visitor to the realm of scientific over-achievement, the studio made a bid to master brain surgery in 1944's *Return of the Ape Man*. Add in equal parts Bela Lugosi, a fresh frozen cave man and that mythical Monogram "mystique," and you have yourself one of the most beloved bad movies of the decade.

Return of the Ape Man unspools in typical mind-numbing Poverty Row fashion. In search of a life form trapped in suspended animation, Professor Dexter (Lugosi) leads an expedition to the Arctic where he finds a perfectly preserved specimen of prehistoric man (Frank Moran). Carted back to Dexter's lab, the Neanderthal-sicle is thawed (with the aid of a blow torch!) and revived. Unfortunately the subject exhibits some deep-seated antisocial behavioral patterns, such as thrashing about the laboratory in an uncontrollable rage. The solution—substitute a portion of the cave dweller's brain with that of modern man, thus serving to "advance his mind 20,000 years in a few hours."

Working with assisting surgeon Professor Gilmore (John Carradine), Dexter elucidates upon his working hypothesis. By replacing a key segment of the primitive subject's brain, he hopes to imprint the creature with speech and reasoning power, while leaving its ancient memories undisturbed. But the self-righteous Gilmore objects, pointing out that this procedure

Bela Lugosi (Professor Dexter), Judith Gibson (Anne) and Frank Moran (Ape Man)

would surely result in the death of the donor. "Murder is an ugly word," deadpans Dexter, in a memorable case of ethical denial. "As a scientist, I do not recognize it."

Recognize it or not, Dexter does not flinch when it comes to doing the dirty work. Finger-pointing Gilmore becomes the eventual victim, rendered prostrate by Dexter's electrically charged booby trap. After the operation, the ape man shows impressive progress, demonstrating a limited capacity for speech ("Me…Gilmore," he grunts repeatedly), the ability to tinkle a tune on the piano and a somewhat more docile disposition. Dangerous, primitive instincts still lurk beneath the surface, however, as evidenced by the beast's murder of Gilmore's wife, when the lady issues a startled scream (a perfectly understandable reaction given her husband's sudden change in appearance). Needless to say, Dexter's highfalutin plans to turn his discovery into a "righteous citizen" quickly fall asunder.

Return of the Ape Man abounds with those wonderfully incongruous moments that exist only in the world of Monogram. With its laugh-out-loud dialogue ("You know," muses Dexter while perusing a dinner party of potential victims, "some people's brains would never be missed"), absurd images (Lugosi parading around the town with flaming blow torch in hand) and ridiculous premise, the film specializes in entertainment value of the lowest kind. In regards to the brain procedure, however, things are handled earnestly enough. Incorporated into the story at just the right moment to ratchet the horror content upward, the gambit is a patented example of the studio's weird-for-weird's-sake approach to fright cinema. Of course not everyone can appreciate it, but in films like these, Monogram left a mark with its distinctive, bargain-basement style. Hey, where else can you glimpse a Neanderthal man giving a recital of Beethoven's "Moonlight Sonata?"

By contrast, 1944 also brought us a more respectable treatment of brainwork in Republic's *The Lady and the Monster*. Adapted somewhat loosely from Curt Siodmak's successful novel *Donovan's Brain*, the film eschews straightforward transplantation in favor of the mystic razzle-dazzle of psychic telepathy. But with its dark look, quasi-mad scientist and

Professor Mueller (Erich von Stroheim) and his delightful mad lab, with Janice (Vera Ralston) in the foreground

laboratory brimming over with technical accoutrements, *Lady* does indeed fit comfortably into the 1940s catalog of brain borrowers.

In a Gothic castle deep in the Arizona desert (!), Professor Franz Mueller (Erich von Stroheim) is researching the possibility of keeping brain tissue alive past the point of death. Assisted by Dr. Patrick Corey (Richard Arlen) and Janice Farell (Vera Hruba Ralston), Mueller's work is confined to animal experiments, until that lucky night when a private plane crashes nearby. No angst-ridden soul-searching for this wacky medico—no sooner than you can say "anesthesia," he instructs Corey to bring a dying victim back to the lab, presumably in an effort to save the patient's life. But when fate does not cooperate, Mueller quickly shifts gears and has the still-functioning brain removed and wired up to a life-sustaining apparatus.

Placed on display like a tabletop centerpiece, the tissues continue to exhibit normal brain waves. To establish communication, the doctor hits upon the notion of telepathy. All they need is "…someone who can make his own mind an absolute blank." (At this point, von Stroheim shoots Arlen a look that is absolutely priceless.) *The Lady and the Monster* remains noticeably vague concerning the particulars of this process. Does successful telepathy depend on an abnormally powerful transmitting organ or will any old household brain do? In any case, after supplying a healthy overdose of blood plasma, Corey soon finds himself attuned to the brain's thought patterns like a well-configured satellite dish.

But the thinking machine proves to have a mind of its own. Formerly the province of business magnate William H. Donovan, it begins to establish its dominion over its host in hopes of freeing the tycoon's convicted son, who awaits the electric chair for a murder that his father committed. Complications arise also when Donovan's attorney puts two and two together and infers the true nature of Mueller's research work. In true Republic fashion, the film concludes with a rock 'em, sock 'em showdown, which results in the brain being usurped from its temporary position of power.

The Lady and the Monster spends far too much time on the soap opera histrionics of Arlen and former skating queen Ralston (who does absolutely nothing to justify her star billing). But the film has its moments—its shadowy atmosphere is

Reel Mad Doctors

reasonably effective and von Stroheim's obsessed scientist, played with a gimpy gait and pit bull obstinacy, is a treat to watch. Like many of the movies mentioned in this overview, *Lady* depicts brain domination in Jekyll and Hyde fashion. While under the control of Donovan's mind, Corey undergoes a distinct personality shift (visually reinforced by dramatic frontal lighting). Only when the brain is doped with morphine does Corey once again regain control over his own faculties. They say that two heads are better than one, but on the basis of *The Lady and the Monster,* we are forced to conclude that one is certainly more than sufficient.

A second take on *Donovan's Brain* was filmed in 1953. Retaining the story's original title, the film is likewise considerably more faithful in its adaptation of the story line. While violating the parameters of this article ever so slightly, this bridge between 1940s science fantasy and 1950s neo-realism provide a highly satisfying finale to the prior decade's ongoing brain sagas.

Donovan's Brain eschews the Gothic trappings of *The Lady and the Monster* for a more realistic approach. In this adaptation, Pat Cory (Lew Ayres) heads up the research, assisted by wife Janice (Nancy Davis, who displays the same plastic grin that would become her trademark as First Lady) and local doctor/struggling alcoholic Frank Schratt (Gene Evans). The crash of Donovan's plane again sets the story

Dr. Corey (Lew Ayres) and Dr. Schratt (Gene Evans) examine the brain in the tank, in *Donvan's Brain* (1953).

in motion, although this version introduces a complication in the person of freelance writer Yocum (Steve Brodie), who connives his way into Cory's lab and takes a snapshot of the illicitly obtained brain. Cory, for the most part, is considerably more down to earth than the prior brain researchers we have seen, although his eyes still light up like a kid at Christmas when caught up in his latest pet project.

Clairvoyance is once again the medium by which Cory connects, and then succumbs, to the mind of Donovan. The dominance is gradual and subtle; devoid of any special effects, Cory's change is made evident by a slight but noticeable limp, symptomatic of Donovan's chronic kidney ailment. While more believable than the "all or nothing" transformation seen in other films, this change does result in a few eyebrow-raising moments, as when nice guy Ayres begins to bark out instructions to attorneys, bank managers and government investigators with a seemingly misplaced sense of authority.

Cory is gradually drawn into the unresolved circumstances of Donovan's life as the domination progresses. Increasing in power, the brain spontaneously generates the ability to dominate others on a one-at-a-time basis, exerting its influence over Yocum with deadly consequences. By film's finale, the brain of Donovan is on the verge of becoming an unstoppable, self-sufficient entity, save for instructions left by Cory in one of those rare moments when he was still functioning as his own man.

Donovan's Brain stands out as the best of this batch of brainteasers. Credible performances aid immensely—players Ayres and Evans lend a verisimilitude that transcends the overly sensational elements of the story. The movie's straightforward approach (typical of fantastic films from this decade) also helps to tilt the needle on the believability meter. As a final footnote, it is truly bizarre to watch actress Nancy Davis in the days when Ronald Reagan was still a registered Democrat. Hey, wait a minute. Given the subject matter of *Donovan's Brain*, you don't suppose that…No, let's not go there.

By this time, meddling with the human brain had become firmly entrenched as the type of cinematic bromide that would find its way into the two-reelers of The Three Stooges. Come the 1950s and 1960s, brains would routinely be featured as a key element in a series of "weird science" movies, often with space invader overtones. From *Fiend Without A Face* (1957), *The Brain Eaters* (1958), *The Brain From Planet Arous* (1958), *The Thing That Couldn't Die* (1958), *The Man Without A Body* (1959), *The Brain* (a.k.a. *Vengeance,* 1962, yet another retelling of the durable Siodmak tale), *The Brain That Wouldn't Die* (1962) to *They Saved Hitler's Brain* (1963), filmmakers resolutely followed the lead of this first round of brain pioneers, confirming the filmic possibilities offered by the human thinking machine.

So heads up, all you potential neurosurgeons out there! These films provide an excellent way to begin your apprenticeship. Hidden behind the sometimes hoary plots and convoluted dramatics are invaluable clues to understanding the mechanics of basic brain manipulation. The next time you are up to your elbows in cranial cavities and cerebral tissue, remember that wacky, wonderful decade of the 1940s where it all began.